Commentary on
Michigan Indian Boarding School Survivors Speak Out

"A thoroughly researched, thoughtfully presented discussion of one of the dark sins of America: the Indian Boarding Schools. The interviews with nine Northern Michigan residents telling how their times in these schools deeply affected the rest of their lives are deeply moving."
—Jon C. Stott, author of *Native Americans in Children's Literature*

"Sharon Brunner is a prolific writer who uses her Native American roots to write stories that speak of the trauma Indigenous people experience as a result of being forced to live in Christian boarding schools. Children were taken from their families, their culture, and their roots. Brunner's true stories are written with a passion that flows from deep within her."
—Sharon Kennedy, *EUP News*

"Sharon Marie *Brunner's Michigan Indian Boarding School Survivors Speak Out* is meticulously researched and a recommended reading for the serious student of Native American history. The author focuses on the accounts of nine former boarding school residents and the effects their experiences had on their lives and on the lives of their descendants. Especially appreciated is the author's detailed background presentation against which she weaves these personal narratives. Reading this book is helping me as I research my grandfather's story."
—Ann Dallman, freelance journalist and author of the award-winning *Cady Whirlwind Thunder* mystery series.

"In *Michigan Indian Boarding School Survivors Speak Out*, Brunner provides an unprecedented and systematic discussion with first-person accounts of multifarious abuses to the boys and girls consigned to these institutions. The fact that many were able to resist and overcome this soul-crushing experience is a tribute to the resilience of the human spirit."
—Victor Volkman, *Marquette Monthly*

"As an Australian political activist, I have been campaigning for justice for my country's First Nations people. Therefore, Sharon Brunner's account of the sufferings of Native Americans in much the same way, during much the same times, spoke to my heart. It is essential for all of us to know about the genocide, disdain, cultural destruction, and discrimination heaped on all the original inhabitants of the lands Europeans stole. The book is based on Sharon's qualitative research, and in addition gives a useful literature survey. I can recommend it to anyone with empathy and a sense of justice."

—Robert Rich, PhD

Michigan Indian Boarding School Survivors Speak Out

A Narrative History

Sharon Marie Brunner

Modern History Press

Ann Arbor, MI

Michigan Indian Boarding School Survivors Speak Out: A Narrative History
Copyright © 2024 by Sharon Marie Brunner. All Rights Reserved

ISBN 978-1-61599-802-9 paperback
ISBN 978-1-61599-803-6 hardcover
ISBN 978-1-61599-804-3 eBook

Cover image: Holy Childhood of Jesus Indian School, Harbor Springs, MI. Courtesy of Harbor Springs Historical Society.

Published by
Modern History Press   info@ModernHistoryPress.com
5145 Pontiac Trail   www.ModernHistoryPress.com
Ann Arbor, MI 48105

Library of Congress Cataloging-in-Publication Data

Names: Brunner, Sharon Marie, 1957- author.
Title: Michigan Indian boarding school survivors speak out : a narrative history / Sharon Marie Brunner.
Description: Ann Arbor, MI : Modern History Press, [2024] | Includes bibliographical references. | Summary: "Brunner's social work research into Michigan Indian Boarding Schools led her to gather oral histories from nine Native American survivors of the Mt. Pleasant Indian Industrial Boarding School and the Holy Childhood of Jesus School in Harbor Springs. Analysis of the themes reveals the cruelties inflicted by the Boarding School system including starvation, corporal punishment, and sexual abuse of minors"-- Provided by publisher.
Identifiers: LCCN 2024012699 (print) | LCCN 2024012700 (ebook) | ISBN 9781615998029 (paperback) | ISBN 9781615998036 (hardcover) | ISBN 9781615998043 (epub)
Subjects: LCSH: Mount Pleasant Indian Industrial School--History--20th century. | Holy Childhood Boarding School--History--20th century. | Off-reservation boarding schools--Michigan--History. | Indians, Treatment of--Michigan--History. | Oral history.
Classification: LCC E97.5 .B78 2024 (print) | LCC E97.5 (ebook) | DDC 977.4/00497--dc23/eng/20240409
LC record available at https://lccn.loc.gov/2024012699
LC ebook record available at https://lccn.loc.gov/2024012700

Survivors of the
Michigan Indian Boarding School Experience Speak Out

"There was a girl that went to school there (Holy Childhood Boarding School) and knew not a word of English. They beat her if she would talk in her language. She would hang her head. My dad said the same thing. He would not teach us. When I heard an elder speaking the language, it took me right back to when I was a kid."

—Yulanda

"We moved here (Sault Ste. Marie, MI) because of the situation then, it wasn't good to be an Anisaahnabe. So, my aunts were anything but Anishaanabe. They were French. They were Italian. They were anything anybody that kind of had a dark color to their skin. That's what they had. They wouldn't hire my uncles at Algoma Steel or any place like that because they were Anishaanabe... It's like the language. They couldn't speak their own language. They could speak French. The French were accepted but people still looked down their noses at the French a little bit. English was the A number one thing."

—Kent

"We really starved. Breakfast, I don't know what that was that they gave us but there was no sugar or cream on it or anything. Bugs were in it, and they would make us eat that...I don't remember ever having a decent meal down there."

—Brenda

"They took you in front of everybody, laid you across the bed and used a rubber hose. As young as you were, when you wet the bed..."

—Jennifer

"I have more hair on the left side of my head than I do the right because they would drag me around by the hair. The hair was pulled out of my head. Plus, they would grab you by the hair and slam you into the chalkboard. I was up close to the chalkboard a lot of the times."

—Yulanda

"I would have much rather been at home where Mom and Dad were fighting, drinking and there was domestic violence... than to go through being institutionalized in a place where they tell you that you're evil. You're totally evil and nothing is ever going to save you. So, you may as well give yourself over to God and die however that God deems, because if you don't the devils got you, fear of the devil. What they made me afraid of was the dark."

—Tim

"She grabbed a board and beat me with that board... Why don't you hit me back. I was always respectful to older people... She really wanted me to cry. I would not cry. It was not until I was in bed alone that I cried."

—Yulanda

"Things happened to our ancestors that devastated them. That was supposed to destroy us. But it didn't totally destroy us, but it sure did a lot of damage. We have had four to five hundred years of this kind of treatment. The dysfunctions that are rampant in our families, the addictions... It was designed to really break you down. Make you into something different."

—Tim

"The government expected the Indian to farm. They didn't know anything about farming... They put the reserve on the poorest land... But I remember my dad coming up the road with a big steelhead, the tail of the fish dragging in the sand... He hunted, but hunting was poor. Game was scarce."

—Jeff (Mt. Pleasant Boarding School)

"Lieutenant Peterson was a real American Company C... I was at attention, and he stood right in front of me and he said *private* and I said *yes sir... Did you ever go to West Point? Where did you get your training at?* I said that I went to a government Indian school in Mt. Pleasant, Michigan."

—Fred (Mt. Pleasant Boarding School)

This is dedicated in the memory of
all the Native Americans who suffered as a result of
the oppression of the European Americans.

Megwetch Gitchi Manitou (Thanks Creator)
for your guidance during this project.

Contents

Acknowledgements 1

Chapter 1 - About the Study 3

    Introduction 3

    Purpose of Study 6

    Operational Definitions 8

    Theoretical Overview 10

    Social Learning Theory 10

    Pedagogy of the Oppressed 11

    Shame 11

    Standpoint Theory 13

    Ethnostress 14

    Historical Trauma: 15

Chapter 2 – Literature Review 25

    PreColonialism: (Traditional Period) 25

    The Plight of Native Americans in Michigan After the European Invasion 27

    The History of Indian Boarding Schools 38

    Mt. Pleasant Boarding School 47

        Historical Background 47

    Holy Childhood School in Harbor Springs 49

        Historical Background 49

    Comparison of Teaching and Learning Practices 51

    Abyss and Revitalization Period: (Twentieth Century): 54

    Twenty-first Century: Establish a U.S. Truth and Healing Commission 62

Chapter 3 – Methodology 65

Chapter 4 – Results 71

    Oral Historical Accounts 71

        Mt. Pleasant Boarding School 71

        Interview #1: Jeff from Haslett, Michigan 71

        Interview # 2: Doris from Sault Ste. Marie, Michigan 75

        Interview # 3: Fred from Sault Ste. Marie, Michigan. 77

    Holy Childhood Boarding School 80

        Interview #4: Kent from Sugar Island 80

        Interview #5: Yulanda from Petoskey 84

        Interview #6 Brenda from St. Ignace 89

        Interview #7: Tim from Sault Ste. Marie, Michigan 91

        Interview #8: Jennifer from St. Ignace 95

        Interview #9: Diane from St. Ignace 97

    Individual Interview Analysis 101

    Summary of Results 110

Chapter 5 – Discussion 113

    Importance Placed on Involvement with Family and Friends .. 113

    Traditional Cultural Practices 114

    Ojibwe Language (Anishaanabemowin) 115

    Lived on a Reservation 115

    Multigenerational Attendance of Boarding Schools 116

    Alcoholism 116

    Domestic Violence 116

    Poverty 116

    Court Ordered/Parents' Personal Choice to Send Child(ren) to the Boarding School 117

    Aggression Toward Other Children 118

Michigan Indian Boarding School Survivors iii
   Harsh Discipline and Censored Communication/Fears and Phobias 118
   Mixed Messages About Religion 119
   Expressed Feelings of Abandonment 119
   Regimented Teaching and Monitoring Practices at the Boarding Schools 120
   Institutionalization/Materialism 120
   Institutionalization/Disciplined Behaviors 120
   Developed Alliances with Other Children and Adults 121
   Resistance to Authority 122
   Identity Confusion 122
   Resentments Stated About Being Sent to the Boarding School 123
   Summary of Discussion 124
   Implications for Further Research 124
   Additional Questions for Future Studies 125

Chapter 6 – Implications of the Study 127
   Implications for Social Work Practice: (Individual and Family, Community and National Perspectives) 128
      Individual and Family Perspective 128
      Community Perspective 130
      National Perspective 131

Chapter 7 – Measuring the Impacts 133
   Depression and Suicide: 133
   Alcohol and Substance Abuse 133
   Health Disparities 133
   Transportation 135
   Education Disparities 135

Appendix 1 – Legends 137
   The First Porcupine 137
      First Legend 137

Second Legend 138

Appendix 2 – History of Federal Indian Education Policy 139

Appendix 3 – Indian Affairs Head Apologized for Agency's Legacy of Racism 143

Appendix 4 – Informed Consent Form 145

Appendix 5 – Research Questions 147

Appendix 6 – History of the Meriam Report 149

Appendix 7 – The Doctrine of Discovery 153

Bibliography 155

About the Author 167

Acknowledgements

I would like to express my gratitude to the members of my masters thesis committee, Dr. Jane Swanson, Chairperson, Mr. Martin Reinhardt, and Dr. Jerry Johnson for their support and guidance on this project. I would like to thank Mr. Robert VanAlstine for his provision of valuable materials and insight. And a sincere thank you to the interview participants for sharing their accounts of their family history and boarding school experience. Many resources provided me valuable information to enable me to complete a literature review and other parts of this project. I also want to thank my family who tolerated my involvement in this process. I hope to provide insight to the strengths and difficulties still endemic in the lives of the Anishinaabek.

Chapter 1 – About the Study

Prophecy

We knew this is the wealthiest part of this continent, because here the Great Spirit lives. We knew that the White Man will search for the things that look good to him, that he will use many good ideas in order to obtain his heart's desire, and we knew that if he had strayed from the Great Spirit he would use any means to get what he wants. These things we were warned to watch, and we today know that those prophecies were true because we can see how many new and selfish ideas and plans are being put before us. We know that if we accept these things, we will lose our land and give up our very lives.
-Dan Katchongva, Hopi American Indian

Introduction

The Native American population have continued to face a multitude of problems such as high rates of suicide, substance abuse, depression, and poverty, as a possible result of the boarding school legislation and other acts of oppression. I was drawn to learn more about boarding schools and how they may have affected Native Americans and their culture, because my mother and her siblings were forced to attend the Holy Childhood boarding school in Harbor Springs, Michigan. Questions came to the forefront concerning the boarding schools. Was their experience similar to others who attended? Did the boarding schools and other acts of oppression cause many of the problems Native Americans currently encounter? The twenty-three years I spent on the Child Welfare Committee for the Sault Ste. Marie Tribe of Chippewa Indians of which I am a member has revealed a multitude of problems Native American families experienced, which predominantly involved substance abuse along with child abuse and neglect. Did these families have a history of attending the boarding schools? Did the grandparents of the children represented at the meetings attend the boarding schools? The history of the Native Americans was laced with multiple forms of abuse from boarding schools, to being placed on reservations, infected with deadly diseases and their land having been taken away. Even their right to practice their spiritual beliefs was taken away for approximately 100 years. The study revealed interesting information while it delved into the aftereffects of the boarding school experience.

I discovered that my paternal grandfather spoke fluent Anishanaabemowin (Ojibwe language) and French as well as English. His mother spoke Anishanaabemowin and broken English. When he was a child, the Jesuits moved into my grandfather's childhood home to convert them to Christianity. My maternal grandfather's family moved to St. Ignace. I am not sure when this move occurred. My grandfather stayed in his family of origin's home to care for his mother after his father passed away. He was older when he met my grandmother at the time they married. The birth of their children occurred soon after that. My mother's family of origin went through hard times. Jobs were scarce in St. Ignace and if you claimed to be a Native American, you could not get a job. My grandfather had to claim to be French. They survived problems such as substance abuse, and loss of employment. The "Depression" caused hardship for the family, who suffered from near starvation and had to obtain free clothing and other assistance.

Meanwhile, my grandparents' children, which included my aunts, uncles, and mother were placed in the Holy Childhood Boarding School in Harbor Springs, Michigan, and other relatives' homes because of their inability to care for them. Some of my uncles spent time in reform schools because of their unruliness. My mother told me my grandfather and some of my uncles had difficulty controlling their anger. My mother said she went through periods of rage as a teenager.

I was born and raised in St. Ignace, Michigan. Many of the people in the community had a strong dislike for Native American people. I remember they were referred to as "dirty useless Indians." When I was seventeen, my mother obtained tribal identification cards for herself and her children. All along I had thought I was French and Dutch. I went along with this confusing situation but felt slighted, like I missed out on a lot. My mother and other family members searched to find documents such as death and birth certificates that explained our family's lineage.

In 1987, I began working for the Sault Ste. Marie Tribe of Chippewa Indians. I was employed as a secretary for the Binogii (child) Placement Agency until I took a position as an Education Coordinator for the Sault Tribe Johnson O'Malley Program., My interest in my Native American heritage was sparked considerably at this time. An elder took me under her wing and taught me part of the language, and instructed me in areas of interest such as powwow etiquette. I shared this information with the children in the classrooms in St. Ignace.

Around this period, my mother was introduced to the sweat lodge ceremony. She convinced me to go with her. I was scared and did not know what to expect. The people at the lodge welcomed me and told me to just let things happen. This and subsequent experiences at the sweat lodge have been extremely gratifying. They have taught me how to take care of myself and my family and how to find balance in my life.

As a Native American, it has been upsetting to learn about my ancestors and how they have been led to believe they were worthless and inferior because of their Native American lineage. My ancestors denied their heritage in order to fit as peacefully as possible into communities where various forms of discrimination were practiced against Native American people.

This project involved meeting with people who attended two boarding schools: the Federal Boarding School in Mt. Pleasant, Michigan, and the Holy Childhood Boarding School in Harbor Springs, Michigan. I did not meet with people who attended the boarding school in Baraga, Michigan. The interview participants provided me with valuable information about their boarding school experience. The Federal Boarding School closed in 1933, and I was fortunate to meet with three attendees. I felt elated that these three people agreed to share their experiences with me.

The terms used to define the tribal people with this project were Native Americans, indigenous, Indians, Indian people, the Anishanaabek (original people) or native people. The word "Indian" was derived from Columbus' first encounter with people from the Western Hemisphere. He called them "Una gente in Dios," a people in God. Therefore, the given name of Indian was a perfectly noble and respectable word. People of European descent were referred to as Europeans, Euro-Americans, White Americans, European Americans, white settlers, and Anglo-invaders.

The Native Americans and European Americans have resided in the United States together for hundreds of years. The United States was born as the result of the indigenous nations losing a vast amount of their land, the advanced weaponry of the European Americans, Christian missionaries, deadly diseases, and a multitude of laws such as the boarding school legislation. It has been noted in other sources that the boarding school legislation has caused more damage than any other acts of oppression. The study of the aftereffects of the boarding school experience for Native Americans in Michigan revealed a lot of this damage.

This study focused on the family history and boarding school experience of nine Native Americans in the state of Michigan. Primary questions were utilized to gain information regarding perseverance and problems still being faced in 2001, which may have been associated with their boarding school experience. Interview participants were selected who attended the Mt. Pleasant and Holy Childhood boarding schools. These individuals reported both negative and positive recollections about their boarding school experiences. Themes were derived from the interview summaries and utilized for the analysis portion of this project. The results revealed similarities and differences between the experiences of those who attended both institutions. An extensive literature review was conducted. This thesis was designed to be useful for social workers, educators, and others when implementing services and developing policy that addresses the unique challenges and strengths of Native American people.

Purpose of Study

The purpose of this study involved the exploration of the aftereffects of the boarding school phenomena, and to learn more about the factors that have led to the perseverance exhibited by many Native American people and how these factors were related to their boarding school experience. Steadfast resilience was demonstrated by many of these Native American children. They continued to struggle with holding onto their cultural identity. They did so by various acts of resistance, and by forming alliances. As a result, they maintained a sense of autonomy against an oppressive system, the boarding school institutions (Littlefield, 1989).

Assimilation into the European Americans' way of life served as the main goal for the development of the boarding school institutions (Tyler, 1973). Problems such as alcoholism and racism have been endemic in the lives of many Native American people for a very long time, before the implementation of the aforementioned institutions (Antone, Miller, and Myers, 1986). These hardships may have been symptoms of the boarding school experience. Theoretical perspectives have explained the rationale behind the behaviors exhibited by the Native Americans and European Americans and how these behaviors were associated to the possible aftereffects of the prisons labeled boarding schools.

Operational Definitions

The raw data analyzed for this project were placed into theme categories. Some of the areas covered are not self-explanatory. Definitions were given for areas that may appear ambiguous for the reader.

Assimilation: The process in which individuals or groups from a different ethnic heritage are absorbed into the dominant culture and adopt their customs.

Alliances Developed with Adults and Children: Children formed social support systems while attending the boarding schools. Some of them maintained these friendships into their adulthood.

Censored Communication: Letters written by the students at the boarding schools to be sent to their parents were monitored. The students had to change the letters if they contained information that was deemed inappropriate, especially if it could implicate the adults at the boarding schools of any wrongdoing.

Epistemology of the Family of Origin: Interview participants gave testimony of the nature of their family of origin to the best of their recollection. The central concepts they remembered included poverty, involvement with friends and family, abandonment, and alcoholism.

Harsh Discipline: This form of discipline consisted of cruel and severe punishment. Beatings with a rubber hose were an example of this (Littlefield, 1989).

Identity Confusion: Many Native American people struggled with self-doubt concerning their personal identity related to their tribal heritage. Native American children were placed in these foreign environments and their cultural development thwarted during a crucial period in their lives (Fixico, 2000).

Institutionalized: Many children carried learned behaviors from the boarding school experience into adulthood. They became conditioned to follow the regimented lifestyle instilled during their stay at the institutions. A goal of the boarding school experience was to assimilate children into the European American culture, which included values such as a materialistic point of view.

Mixed Messages About Religion: The children were provided religious instruction and at the same time treated in a manner that contradicted the religious lessons they were being taught.

Parent's Personal Choice to Send Their Child(ren) to the Boarding Schools: Multiple childbirths, poverty, mental health issues such as depression as a result of oppression, and substance abuse were some of the reasons why parents sent their children to the boarding schools.

Perseverance: Many Native American children continued the struggle of holding onto their cultural identity. They did so by their demonstration of various acts of resistance and by forming alliances. As a result, they maintained a sense of autonomy against an oppressive system (Littlefield, 1989).

Regimented Teaching and Monitoring Practices: One of the main goals of the boarding schools was to teach Native American children to follow orders. Students were expected to march in line and participate in military-style drills. A strict schedule was set up for daily tasks. Adults and older students provided the monitoring of assigned roles and responsibilities. Children were disciplined if rules were not followed, sometimes severely (Littlefield, 2001).

Resilience: The ability to recover quickly from adversity.

Resistance to Authority: Students attempted to undermine the authority imposed on them while staying at the boarding schools. They recounted episodes in which food was stolen, and of times when they left the boarding school buildings to explore, fish, and other activities during the nighttime hours. Running away was another example (Littlefield, 1989).

Traditional Cultural Practices: The term "culture" refers to values, beliefs, and worldviews that lend an explanation to people's behaviors. The traditional cultural practices represented the socialized ideals within tribal societies before the arrival of European Americans. These were learned through the use of language and other forms of instruction. Storytelling was an example of this and was utilized to provide important lessons (Haviland, 1994).

Theoretical Overview

Boarding schools were established during a time when the European American inhabitants were colonizing parts of this country. (Refer to Appendix 2 for Chronology of Related Events.) Resources were needed for these inhabitants. Traditional Native American homelands encompassed some of the most valuable land. Many tribes were nomadic. They moved from place to place to find game, fish and suitable land for farming and gathering. Sometimes tribes needed to relocate during inclement weather to seek shelter from the natural elements. The reservations, boarding schools, and other methods of assimilation have caused many problems for Native American people. A land of opportunity for the European Americans soon became a land of oppression for those here before them (Bowden, 1981). Today, Native Americans continue to be faced with the aftermath of this disruption of their traditional lifestyles.

In this thesis, I examined and analyzed the boarding school experience by the utilization of various social learning theoretical perspectives and theories based on power and control. These theories were subsequently used to analyze how and why boarding schools were established and the effect these institutions had on the ones who attended.

Behavior does not occur in a vacuum without internal and external forces. Humans have always been products of their environments. Children have been trained to follow directions. Reinforcing conditions and personality constructs were byproducts. Behavior was a sum of these two components (Rotter, et al., 1972). When children were beaten for speaking their language, they began to believe their safety was far more important than their cultural heritage. Children were sometimes given gifts when they learned some of the European American ways. A variety of theories were utilized to analyze the aftereffects of this personal history.

Social Learning Theory

Learning has occurred through modeling. Modeling led to three kinds of effects while observing others. These effects delineate different aspects of aggression. Observation can result in the acquisition of new patterns of behaviors. Modeling influences either strengthen or weaken inhibitions of behavior for those observing. The observers may have been previously educated by rewarding and punishing consequences closely associated with inhibitory and disinhibitory effects (Bandura, 1973). Many Native American families continue to face problems that involve domestic violence, child abuse and neglect, coupled with substance abuse. These factors tear at the embracing fabric of families (Anton, Miller and Myers, 1986). Many children either witnessed and/or were the victims of child abuse at the boarding schools. They learned how to parent by observing the boarding school staff.

Pedagogy of the Oppressed

The nature of the European American people led to their attempt at cultural domination through the public education system. This "sadistic drive" (p. 59) was the result of multigenerational conditioning. Domination, through the use of education and violence by those with power, oppressed those without power. Both groups were influenced by the repetitive process of domination. Over time, the dominant culture developed a possessive consciousness, which became the identity of the individual. Oppressors found pleasure in the act of transforming the animate into the inanimate, taking away the freedom essential for a sustained quality of life (Freire, 1993). However, in the act of oppressing others, they oppressed themselves.

This in turn led to a lack of cultural authenticity of the Native American people. They could not openly oppose the control inflicted on them by the European Americans. This correlated with the "culture of silence." The adoption of the European American culture weakened their association with their own cultural heritage. One of the main goals of the European Americans was to condition the Native Americans to accept and adopt their patterns and way of life. They studied the Native American people to the extent necessary to gather an understanding of what values and other concepts were of the most importance to them, which permitted them to exert dominance more effectively (Freire, 1993).

Shame

Shame, a conscious emotion, was developed as a result of feelings of unworthiness, that something was fundamentally wrong concerning an individual. When people made others feel ashamed, they lost honor and respect. Native Americans throughout history have been treated like they were less than human, and undeserving of respect. The staff at the boarding schools told the children they were heathens and evil and had to convert to Christianity and adopt the European American ways to save themselves. Their traditional way of life came into question.

The seven main sources of shame included: faulty learning, excessive negative feedback, poor decision-making, being a victim of circumstance, false identity, inaccurate perceptions, and loss of social status or recognition. In regard to faulty learning, sometimes the wrong information was received or untrue information was believed to be true. Excessive negative feedback referred to being told on several occasions they were unworthy or incompetent. An inability to believe in one's capabilities led to difficulty concerning making sound decisions. Being the victim of circumstance made reference to someone whom expected bad circumstances to continue because they had occurred in the past. This was associated with the feelings of constant gloom and doom about the future. Individuals developed false identities when they changed themselves to what they think others wanted them to be. Inaccurate perceptions were in reference to denial and being naïve. Individuals defined themselves by the roles and positions in their lives. Losses were often faced in these areas such as the death of a parent or spouse. How the individual chose to adjust to those losses had a major impact concerning the redefinition of their lives (Steffen, 1999).

Many Native American people have been plagued with alcoholism as a means of dealing with the hardships of their lives. One common denominator has existed in regard to addictive behaviors. Addictions have been used to achieve detachment from feelings. Detachment lessened the feelings of pain. They were self-medicating. The progression of their addictions led to feeling more and more detached from shame and other uncomfortable feelings. This suppressed their anxiety. These behavioral symptoms have detrimental effects on self-esteem and self-worth (Steffen, 1999).

Indigenous people have experienced disruption and loss of their culture and had to redefine their roles within the context of their communities and families. The development of chronic shame may have been associated with the long-lasting effect of the assimilation tactics of the European Americans. Such feelings of shame have in turn been linked to feelings of powerlessness, which were often accurate.

Standpoint Theory

Standpoint theory derived from a complex and differentiated basis. Each circumstance, viewed separately from an individual's perspective, may vary from one point of reference to the next and from one point in time to another. This theory was contradictory from the materialistic point of view, which operated under the assumption that one person's analysis or viewpoint remained consistent over time. Human production was closely connected with the development of human knowledge (Welton, 1997). Knowledge was built on the premise that people only know what they have experienced. Experience led to knowledge. People need to not only be observers but active participants in their own lives (Hundleby, 1997).

The concept of power was an important aspect, because it provided a legitimate basis for the organization of communities and the ideals behind community action. Historically, Native American people have been forced to continually negotiate their own environments including the communities in which they reside (Hundleby, 1997).

The boarding school legislation did not occur in a vacuum. At the time, many European Americans worked towards taking care of the "Indian problem" by the implementation of various forms of legislation. Native American spiritual practices were made unlawful for approximately 100 years. "The Department of Interior's 1883 Code of Indian Offenses[1]—de facto laws that applied only to American Indians—punished Indian dances and feasts by imprisonment or withholding food (treaty rations) for up to thirty days. Any medicine man convicted of encouraging others to follow traditional practices was to be confined in the agency prison for not less than ten days or until he could provide evidence that he had abandoned his beliefs." (Zotigh, 2018, para. 4)

Another major intrusion concerning the sovereignty of tribal nations was the Major Crimes Act of 1885, which took away the responsibility of managing law and order in the tribal villages by its

---

[1] https://rclinton.files.wordpress.com/2007/11/code-of-indian-offenses.pdf

members and gave outside forces the determination for punishment concerning acts that may be considered unlawful. This act interfered with traditional peace-keeping practices and opened the door for the intrusion of outsiders. To separate the Native American people from their tribal villages, the General Allotment Act was put into place in 1887. Individual family units were assigned plots of land to farm. They had to agree to live apart from their tribe. To hurt tribal communities further, "The Indian Education Act of 1891 gave the U.S. Commissioner of Indian Affairs authority to control the whereabouts, activities, and treatment of all tribal children," (Wilson, 2018, p. 105). The boarding school legislation was implemented during a period of time when a variety of laws was put into place to drastically change the life of many Native American people.

During the late 1800s, the United States government pursued many efforts to take control of the Native American population. A cohesive mindset among the oppressors set the stage that represented the Standpoint Theory of that time period. The Native American people either fought the oppressors, or developed a sense of hopelessness. The behaviors of the oppressed and oppressors were established as a result of their experiences.

Ethnostress

Ethnostress was caused by a disruption in the development of cultural beliefs and personal identity due to an act or acts committed by the people in power. As a result, it led to other negative experiences through the interactions with their own culture and interaction with people from other cultures (Antone, et al., 1986). Stereotypes have carried a lot of weight in relationship to self-perceptions. They influence social relationships through the creation of an illusion of reality (Rothenberg, 1998). Today, many people have the freedom to express their cultural identity and move beyond past oppressions. However, they have fallen into a trap of internalizing the stereotypes placed on their parents and grandparents (Antone, et al., 1986).

History portrayed Native American people as being forced onto reservations and their livelihoods taken away. Thus, they became reliant on the government to provide for their basic needs such as clothing, food, and shelter. However, other basic social and psychological needs were neglected and pushed aside. These needs included:

- to be seen
- to be heard when they communicate
- to know their communication is accepted and believed
- to know that others have faith and trust in them
- to be allowed to take their place in the world
- to feel secure about, and at peace with themselves
- to feel their existence is not detrimental, but beneficial to the important people in their life (Antone, et al., 1986).

Native American people went through devastating experiences and still feel their aftermath. No longer did they hold a special place and status amongst their people. A multitude of indigenous people have been placed in a desperate situation, not free to practice their beliefs and punished for being different from the European Americans. The more they were told of their lack worth, the more this belief was instilled in their self-concept. Native American people have internalized their oppression, therefore, holding themselves hostage (Antone, et al., 1986).

Historical Trauma

The negative impact of historical trauma still resonates with many Native Americans today. A multitude of Indian people suffer from a whole host of social ills such as higher rates of domestic violence, depression along with other mental health issues, poverty, domestic violence, and substance abuse, more than any other ethnic group in this country. Historical trauma has been an accumulation of traumatic experiences, which have made a negative impact for multiple generations of Indian people that occurred over a long period of time. For over 500 years, physical, emotional, spiritual, and psychological genocide was inflicted on the Native American people.

Soon after European contact, a period referred to as "cultural transition" occurred, and Native Americans were stripped of their social power and cultural authority. As soon as they realized they could not escape the catastrophic events inflicted upon them, they began to adopt "giving up" behavioral patterns. They withdrew socially, which in turn lessened their social and psychological investment in all their relationships, personally and with their communities.

As a result of the cultural and social disruption, they engaged in destructive behaviors and social alienation. They developed serious psychological problems, such as alcoholism, drug addiction, and other forms of displaced re-enactments of conflict. These disparaging behaviors were acquired as a result of various acts of oppression, which left a legacy of recurring dysfunction and disturbing behavioral patterns associated with cultural disruption.

Imagine the difficulty children faced when they were forced to attend the Indian boarding schools. Many of these children were sexually, emotionally, spiritually, and physically abused. The overall damage inflicted on the children was tremendous. Native Americans, who were forced to attend these institutions and/or reside on reservations, were taught that what happened to them was their fault. They were led to believe they deserved to be abused, and many have lost the ability to trust themselves or others. Because they had no place to turn for safety, their sense of hopelessness grew over time (Eyaa-keen Centre, Inc., 2003).

Historical trauma occurred in six phases:

1. The first contact with the Europeans, which led to a life filled with shock, genocide, no time for grieving, and then the colonization period that introduced disease and alcoholism.

2. The second phase was economic competition between various tribes and their European invaders over resources during the fur trading era and the introduction to a market-based economy. There were physical and spiritual losses experienced during this time period.

3. The European invasion continued involving a war period, which included extermination, and associated refugee problems.

4. Next was a conquest and reservation period, which consisted of forced dependency on their oppressors and a lack of security.

5. The boarding school era destroyed family systems. The infractions involved physical assaults and sexual abuse, along with prohibition of Native languages, spirituality, and cultural associations. The lasting effect includes individuals poorly prepared for parenting their own children. Many Native American people also experienced identity confusion.

6. The final phase of historical trauma consisted of forced relocation to reservations and a termination period, when federally recognized tribal nation status for many tribes was abolished along with the services associated with this status such as food assistance. Many Native Americans perished due to a lack of food and medical services. There was continued prohibition of religious freedom as part of racism and discrimination, and being viewed as second class citizens to the rest of the population. They suffered a loss of a supportive governmental system and a sense of belonging to a community (Eyaa-Keen Centre, Inc., 2003).

The following characteristics represent some of the detrimental effects of historical trauma:

- Helplessness
- Injustice
- A lack of trust
- Feelings of insufficiency
- Toxic shame
- Chronic guilt
- Feelings of brokenness
- A lack of healthy boundaries
- Persistent confusion and frustration
- Isolation and avoidance
- Self-loathing
- Poor Impulse control, which involved alcohol, drugs, eating,

and/or spending

- Maladjusted anger feelings
- Unhappiness and dissatisfaction
- Anxiety disorders, such as Generalized Anxiety Disorder and Post Traumatic Stress Disorder
- Poor communication skills (Stout and Kipling, 2003).

Native Americans' cultural development was severely disrupted by the imposition of Christianity and later on by not knowing how to get their culture back. Today, Native Americans experience glimpses of their cultural identity through exposure to events such as Pow wows and other traditional cultural events, a rare occurrence for far too many. Many of the Indian children who attended the boarding schools came from different tribal groups. However, they were placed in these institutions and treated like they were all the same. Many of these children came from distinctly different Native American cultures. Oftentimes, they did not even share the same native language. The differences created barriers to establishing a sense of connectedness. Language in itself is a very important means of communication with others. The ability to communicate in one's own language as well as the shared commonality of cultural practices was taken away from a multitude of Native American people which caused cultural disturbance.

Cultural disruption has created conditions of:

- Loss of faith and spiritual beliefs
- Internalized stereotypes
- Surviving instead of thriving
- Cultural isolation
- Post Traumatic Stress Disorder and other anxiety issues
- Depression (Stout and Kipling, 2003).

Intergenerational impacts involved a multitude of circumstances such as when the British and French appropriated a vast amount of North American territory and its resources, which in turn instilled further rivalry between opposing tribes due to the shrinking of resources. During the fur trading era, the relationship between European entrepreneurs and the Indians occurred under a drunken haze brought on by the introduction of alcohol to the unsuspecting tribal people. A drunken Indian was easier to steal from and use than a sober one. Indian children were taken from their parents and communities, and placed in cruel and unyielding institutions. Meanwhile, spiritual practices were outlawed so what did the parents of these children do? Many turned to alcohol for their source of comfort.

Acute traumatic events can occur almost anywhere at any time, such as car accidents and natural disasters. Conversely, chronic, long-term trauma occurs only in circumstances of captivity in which the victim or victims are held prisoner. Think about the Native American people who were sequestered to reservations and placed in boarding schools. These children were punished severely if they ran away. As mentioned earlier, physical, psychological and sexual abuse occurred at these institutions on a regular basis.

The captivity of the children in the boarding schools set up a situation of prolonged contact with the perpetrators, creating a special kind of relationship, one based on coercion. The psychological damage of subordination to coercive control has common features such as diminished self-esteem, and depression. The perpetrators such as those in authority at the boarding schools and those placed in control of carrying out the reservation legislation became the most powerful people in the lives of the Indian people. The mindset of the victims has been shaped by the beliefs and actions of the perpetrators. Often little was known about what was behind the beliefs and actions of the perpetrator. However, one common denominator happened to be that the perpetrators believed they were free from assuming any fault concerning any of their wrongdoings. They blamed the victims for any problems or issues.

One of the most disturbing discoveries was that often the perpetrators appeared to be normal to the rest of the world outside the abusive environment. Many sources portrayed perpetrators in prominent positions such as doctors and lawyers. The pedophile priests often appear in the limelight due to their public acts of generosity and good will, which is an idea deeply troubling to most people. For example, Adolf Eichmann during Hitler's reign committed heinous crimes against humanity, but a dozen psychiatrists diagnosed him as normal. Eichmann served as the main drive behind the Holocaust. He organized and managed the arrangements for the deportation of many Jewish people to ghettos and extermination camps (Stout and Kipling, 2003).

The perpetrators are often paranoid, and experience feelings of grandiosity, as if they had the power to possess and conquer the world. They are aware of the realities of power and social norms, so they fit in without being noticed. They seek out situations in which tyrannical behaviors are tolerated, condoned and/or admired. Hitler set the stage for domination of the Jewish people, so Eichmann's behaviors were admired by Hitler and Hitler's devoted followers. The abusive individuals at the boarding schools were able to treat the children as if they were objects undeserving of respect. No one stopped them and the general consensus was that Native Americans in general were undeserving of respect.

Recently, some of Catholic pedophile priests have been punished for their heinous acts. Many of those who ran the prisoner-of-war camps and inflicted harsh treatment on the prisoners had to answer for their crimes. What about the people who wielded harsh treatment on the children at the boarding schools? The government made a formal apology for the treatment of the children who attended the residential schools in Canada. There has been no acknowledgement in the United States concerning the harmful acts wielded upon the Native Americans due to the implementation of reservations and boarding schools.

The perpetrators often demand respect, gratitude, and sometimes love from their victims. For example, the pedophile nuns at the Holy Childhood Boarding School in Harbor Springs, Michigan, often created a simulated loving situation with the boys they were having sexual contact with. They treated the boys as if they were in love with them. Their advances began with kissing the boys and then they brought the boys to their bedrooms to perform sexual acts. Many of the boys felt abandoned when the nuns moved on to other boys.

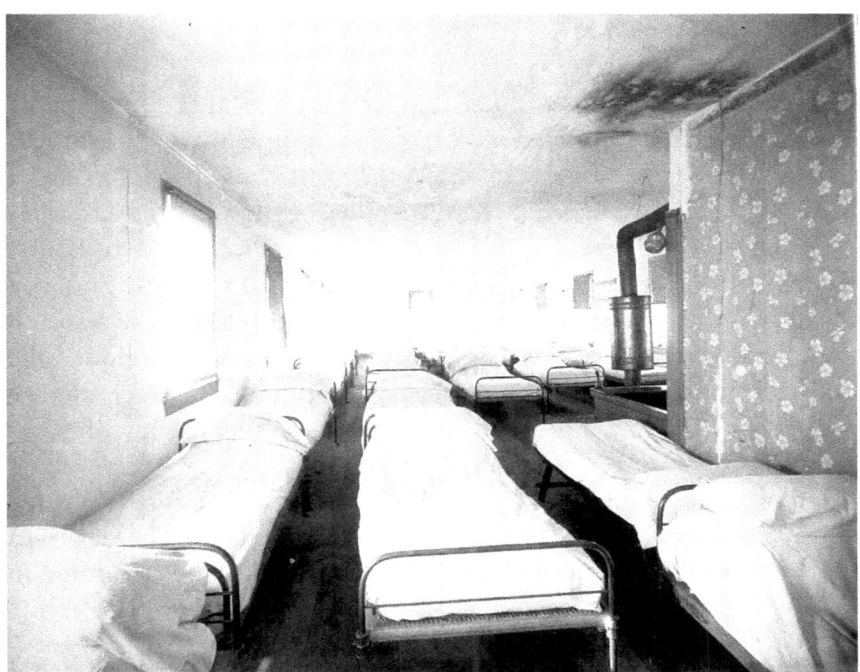

Boys' Dormitory at Harbor Springs (Harbor Springs Historical Society)

One of the first goals of the perpetrators was to enslave the victim(s). They did so by controlling all aspects of the victim's life. But simple obedience demonstrated by the victim was not enough; they moved toward gaining the victim's validation and/or they humiliated the victim in some way. The perpetrators used the victim's feelings of shame to gain even more control over them. Often, the victims lived in constant fear. The children were shown what it was like to not be compliant when they observed other children being physically and emotionally abused in front of them. They were severely punished in front of their peers if they ran away from these cruel institutions. Many of these children were also punished harshly if they were caught speaking their native language.

The children were often underfed at the boarding schools, and a common punishment involved sending them to bed without dinner. This control resulted in physical debilitation through starvation. Along with being hungry most of the time, the children were forced to work extremely hard. They were expected to clean, cook, maintain the grounds, farm, perform other miscellaneous duties, and were also expected to attend school instruction for a few hours a day. They were exhausted, hungry, and abused.

Research has been conducted concerning the aftereffects of the trauma faced by veterans of war. The studies involved how the trauma faced by these veterans effect their offspring. There have been discoveries that the cells within the bodies of the veterans and their offspring contain the memories of the trauma of being on active duty. Many of the Native American people happen to be obese and as a result have been diagnosed with diabetes. Could this be the result of their grandparents' and parents' starvation when they attended the boarding schools or when they faced starvation on the reservations? People often overeat if they don't have a good relationship with food. If food was scarce for their parents and/or grandparents, they took on the scarcity way of thinking, which was passed down from one generation to the next, They overate as a result. The higher levels of obesity within the Native American population may be attributed to the quality of food many could afford (Stout and Kipling, 2003).

Depression, a result of historical trauma that has existed for a multitude of Native Americans, was a common response to oppression, the result of an imbalance of power in relationships. Depression equated to a discrepancy in interpersonal relationships. Depression resulted from anger turned inward, and it also represented unaddressed anger. In other words, depression had arisen in situations in which anger and aggression were suppressed due to fear. A double edged sword has been known to be generated which consisted of suppression of anger and aggression coupled with chronic resentment. This dilemma contributed to internal stress as well as adding to relationship conflicts that in the end fostered additional stress.

Oppression was usually evident in abusive interpersonal relationships such as that between the white settlers and Native Americans throughout history. An extreme accumulation of stress could also become oppressive, which in turn could lead to a response of defeat. The native people often felt trapped after experiencing situations that felt inescapable, not just physically but also psychologically. The intrusive symptoms of painful memories and strong emotions have contributed to a sense of oppression. It was possible to have an oppressive relationship with themselves as a result of past destructive treatment. They may have been the target of their own anger, harsh criticism, and unrealistic demands, adopting a defeated and indignant relationship with themselves. A whole host of problems resulted from self-inflicted oppression as well as from the oppression imposed by others (Stout and Kipling, 2003).

The past of Indian children involved censored and restricted communication while they attended the boarding schools. The children were forced to remain quiet and stare straight ahead. They developed a method of communicating with their eyes when outside of the classroom. They could speak volumes with eye contact amongst their peers. Again, these children were punished, often severely, if they spoke their native language. Speaking became a privilege that could not be practiced for much of the day and into the evening when they were worked on their homework or did chores. Many Native American people may suffer from vast communication barriers as a result of historical trauma.

If Indian children were forced to attend the boarding schools for long periods of time, they discovered that communication with their families of origin was difficult to impossible when they were finally permitted to return to their homes. Trust was one of the main reasons. They were strangers to their families because they were brainwashed into being something they were not, Euro-American replicas, and because of changes during their long stay at these institutions away from their families. Their parents and siblings, who did not have the misfortune of having been separated from their culture, were worlds apart. These children spoke differently, and often their appearance was dissimilar from the rest of their family. They soon discovered they did not fit with their families of origin, usually shortly after moving back home. Thus, many Native American families were literally torn apart. Living on the fringe of both cultural groups and in the effort to belong somewhere, the victims of boarding schools participated in activities that brought them even more shame and feelings of despair.

Historical trauma has taken its toll on many Native Americans. The weapons of mass destruction against the Indian people for centuries have been, but were not limited to: smallpox infestations and other acts of genocide; the introduction of alcohol; broken treaties; forced attendance at boarding schools; enforcement of reservation legislation; and mass sterilization. It has been difficult to determine which losses hurt them the most. With the vast amount of discrimination, it would be amazing if Indian people had any self-esteem at all. To make matters worse when things were in disarray for Native Americans, blame was often placed on the victims.

The aforementioned theoretical perspectives were associated with the assimilation tactics imposed on the Native American people. The policies that put the boarding schools in place were some of those assimilation methods. The adaptation of the Native American people to these acts of assimilation happened to be another important point to consider. Although they represented a small segment of the population in the United States, they have had a disproportionally large number of problems. The history of the Native American people from the precolonial times to the present portrayed their struggles and strengths.

Chapter 2 – Literature Review

PreColonialism: (Traditional Period)

Keepers of the Earth

A long time ago, the Creator came to Turtle island and said to the Red People, "You will be the keepers of the Mother Earth. Among you I will give the wisdom about Nature, about the interconnectedness of all things, about balance and about living in harmony. You Red People will see the secrets of Nature. You will live in hardship and the blessing of this is you will stay close to the Creator. The day will come when you will need to share the secrets with other people of the earth because they will stray from their spiritual ways. The time to start sharing is today.
-Don Coyhis, Mohican Writer and Consultant
American Indian

The Anishinaabek ("the original people") resided in the Great Lakes region. They lived in areas abundant with wild game, fish, and edible plant life such as berries, acorns, and fruit. They did not take this abundance for granted, but had great respect for all of creation. The availability of food afforded the Anishinaabek time to participate in various ceremonies. Villagers danced, sang, played games, participated in family activities, and built the tools they needed for food gathering, farming, and the processing of food and other necessities. They had an optimistic view about life in general and continually planned for their future. A great deal of work was involved in providing sustenance for their families and the community as a whole. The villagers took on the responsibility of ensuring the wellbeing of the community (Clifton, et al., 1986).

They had a system of government called the clan system, which provided strength and order. Seven original clans existed for the Ojibwe people. These were the Crane, Loon, Fish, Bear, Martin, Deer, and Bird. Each served a function for the Anishinaabek. The clan system has continued to be practiced today within various tribal entities to varying degrees. Membership in specific clans was inherited from the father's side. All members of the same clan, blood relatives or not, were considered brothers and sisters. Members of the same clan could not marry (Clifton, et al., 1986). The clan system as well as the kinship network created a blanket of security for the villagers. They expressed a strong commitment to giving and sharing, which was endemic within the tribal communities.

Public speaking was practiced and perfected. The Ojibwe language, which is descriptive, explained human emotions and actions as well as natural phenomena. The speaker vividly recalled events by using their language to instill detailed images. The Anishinaabek were also good listeners. It was considered impolite not to listen, and they considered that important messages could be lost if they did not give their undivided attention to the speaker. Children were strongly encouraged to listen. They were responsible for passing down the traditional information to their children and grandchildren. Children were taught to speak well and portray the exact meanings of what they told others. Stories and legends provided entertainment along with the inclusion of valuable lessons (Clifton et al., 1986).

Children were considered precious gifts provided by the Creator. The entire village provided care, supervision, and instruction to the children (Clifton et al., 1986). Everyone was responsible for the security and protection of the young children. Childbirth was celebrated with feasting and fun activities. The child and mother were inseparable for the first year (Clifton et al., 1986).

The most important event in their life was the receipt of personal identity through a naming ceremony (Johnson, 1990). The given name permitted the child to have a place by the tribal fire and be a part of tribal thoughts. The given name was to be respected for its origin within the tribe and cherished by the one receiving it (Johnson, 1990). Many of the traditional practices have remained a consistent part of the culture of a multitude of Native Americans.

The Anishinaabek provided for themselves by hunting, gathering and fishing, and respected Mother Earth. The communal form of living afforded all of the needs for their villages. They celebrated births, honored given names, gave importance to storytelling and held a kinship network in high esteem. It took an entire village to raise each child to adulthood.

The invasion of the Europeans greatly changed the lives of the Anishinaabek.

The Plight of Native Americans in Michigan After the European Invasion

Spiritual Security

They do us no good. If they are not useful to the white people and do them no good, why do they send them among the Indians? If they are useful to the white people and do them good, why do they not keep them at home? They [the white men] are surely bad enough to need the labor of everyone who can make them better. These men [the missionaries] know we do not understand their religion. We cannot read their book—they tell us different stories about what it contains, and we believe they make the book talk to suit themselves. If we had no money, no land and no country to be cheated out of, these black coats would not trouble themselves about our good hereafter. The Great Spirit will not punish us for what we do not know.

-Red Jacket, Seneca Orator
American Indian

The Native Americans who resided in what was known as Michigan, encountered an invasion of Europeans who brought the ugliness that existed in Europe with them such as murder and corruption. Anglo-invaders sought the rich natural resources the land had to offer such as beavers. The nomadic groups of indigenous people traveled from one area to the next in search of wild game and abundant fishing opportunities to provide for the needs of their villages. Deer, bear and other wildlife were abundant. The lakes and rivers were filled with fish. The Anglo-invaders sought to make North America their land of financial opportunity at the expense of the indigenous people.

During a migration westward, the Ojibwe traveled with the Odawa and Potawatomi tribes and many settled in Michigan. These three tribes, referred to as the Three Fires, worked together to provide for the needs of all. They utilized similar dialects of the Algonquian language as a mode of communicating with one another. The joint cooperation of the Three Fires Confederacy ensured protection and control over the Three Fires' territorial claims from other tribes such as the Iroquois (Peacock and Wisuri, 2002).

The history of wilderness travel represented an enthralling chapter in American history. From 1634 to 1850, the Michigan fur trade was a prominent business. Control of such trade started when the French, British and Scots took part in the profitable business venture. The trade exploded when the wearing of beaver hats became the new fashion trend for Europeans in Europe. The demand for beaver furs led to extensive trapping of the furry animals by Native Americans during the harshness of northern winters when the fur was the thickest. Many battles were fought over the fur-trading business, especially when the animals sought became vastly depleted in specific locations (Conlan, 1994).

The stories of many Native American people, who turned their lives over to enterprises such as the American Fur Company, were filled with financial loss and other hardships. President Jefferson believed the country was run by white Americans and during that time, the general population strove to rid the country of the "Indian problem." To appease the Americans, Jefferson decided to set up the Indian people to turn over their land holdings by using a market economy. Much of the wild game, overhunted by the white settlers, became scarce in many locations. Native Americans had to rely on the trading posts to meet their needs. In order to pay off the debt they owed to the trading posts, they had to turn over their land. More and more white settlers were moving to this country and using more of the land's rich resources. Trading posts were put up in various locations to entice the Indian people to get their needs met and at the same time accumulate debt (Ambrose, 1996).

Moving from a bartering system to a market economy was difficult for the Native American people. Many were confused about this concept. Bartering was something they practiced and was a form of transaction in which goods or services were exchanged for other goods or services without mediums of exchange such as money. Native Americans believed in the concept of reciprocity, which was not practiced by the Europeans.

Indian people struggled and often perished when faced with European diseases, which threatened the stability of their population. Smallpox was used in biological warfare against a segment of the population unprepared to fight off its lethal properties. In 1763, the British provided the Odawa Indians gifts consisting of three little insulated metal boxes. The Odawa were on a peace mission, returning British soldiers safely to the British settlement in Montreal. Under the direction of Sir Jeffery Amherst, the British instructed the Odawa people to not open the metal boxes they were given until they returned from Montreal to their village near present day Harbor Springs, Michigan. Once the metal boxes were opened, the smallpox virus ran rampant amongst the Odawa. Thousands lost their lives to the dreadful virus. The fur trade and colonization had spread diseases throughout the native population. Much intentional and unintentional exposure to lethal diseases occurred quite often and many Native Americans lost their lives.

"Michigan, and the Great Lakes area, was originally populated by the Potawatomi, Sauk, Fox, Huron, Ottawa, Kickapoo, Ojjbwe—also known as the Chippewa, and Menominee Indians. Some tribes moved on naturally, following their prey, avoiding war, whether with other tribes or European conquerors; others were forced by the U.S. government to leave their native lands. It's a long story of settlement, cultural appropriation and assimilation, war, and a fight for autonomy. Ultimately, it's a tale of control and money" (Brody, 2019, paras. 33).

"It's the beginning of the end for Native American autonomy... as the U.S. began to send in settlers first to upstate New York, then Ohio, and later into Michigan. As white settlers began to settle and inhabit the area, they surrounded the Native Americans, taking their land, food sources, and ultimately, their ability to control their own destiny. Then, they began to be systematically removed from their native lands" (Brody, 2019, para. 47).

Millions of Europeans moved overseas to invade, settle, and rule other countries. When Columbus arrived in the Americas in 1492, there were up to 100 million people living on the continent. After 150 years, there were only 3.5 million. Many died of imported diseases or starvation, or were massacred by the colonizers (Mehta, 2019). "In the case of US settler colonization, land was the primary commodity" (Dunbar-Ortiz, 2014, p 7).

Unknown to the Native Americans, white leaders wanted to lure settlers into the various areas, which reduced the Indian domains, because land ownership served as the tax basis by which the new government was financed. The increased white population reduced hunting grounds. Plans for the development of the new country demanded voters, willing workers, and an infrastructure foreign to the Native Americans (Watson, 2011).

White settler colonialism, as an institution or system, usually required violence or the threat of violence to reach its goals of taking over land. People don't hand over their land, resources, children or futures without a fight, and that fight was met with harsh aggression. While employing the force necessary to accomplish the white settler's expansionist goals, the colonizing command instilled blatant force. The belief that both sides, the white settlers and Native Americans, were equally matched, has confused the nature of the historical ramifications. The Euro-American soldiers were often heavily armed and their weaponry was more advanced. Euro-American colonialism, a part of a capitalist economic globalization effort, was genocidal from the very beginning (Dunbar-Ortiz, 2014).

The new country did not have a solid mechanism in place to have a cohesive federal government until 1787. "So after Congress adjourned in early 1787, delegates from twelve states converged on Philadelphia. Their mission was to create a stronger federal government. The participants included future presidents George Washington and James Madison; Alexander Hamilton, who did more to shape the US government than most presidents; and Benjamin Franklin, the most famous American in the world. As May ended, they went into Independence Hall, closed the shutters, and locked the doors. By the time they emerged in late summer they had created the U.S. Constitution, a plan for welding thirteen states into one federal nation. Once it was approved by the states, its centralizing framework would finally give Congress the authority it needed to carry out the functions of a national government: collecting revenue, protecting borders, extinguishing states' overlapping claims to western territory, creating stable trade policy, and regulating the economy..." (Baptist, 2014, p 9).

Importance, placed on the economy and many actions taken against the Native Americans, was based on the federal funds of the United States. For example: President Lincoln pushed for the creation of the Transcontinental Railroad to aid the nation with transporting goods back and forth from sea to shining sea. Many Indian people lost their lives as a result of the railroad, because American soldiers murdered many of them to secure the building of the railroads. Part of the genocide efforts involved the decimation of the buffalo and many were forced onto reservations where they faced starvation. As early as the fur trading days, fur-traders took advantage of the Native Americans by the introduction of alcohol, in which many native people used to mask the pain of the European invasion. The Europeans introduced a market economy to the western hemisphere, which has caused many indigenous people to suffer from its greedy grip.

Indian warriors served as allies during long destructive wars for the French, British and Americans. Tribal societies suffered greatly as the result of continuous warfare. Tribes lost higher than normal numbers of adult males, and many Indian women were forced to seek marriage partners outside of their tribal group. As a result, Indian ethnicities and cultures became diversified. Oftentimes, when Europeans and their tribal allies attacked villages, everything was burned to the ground, including the crops. The resulting poor diets made Indian people even more susceptible to disease. The Europeans would cut off the food supplies when the wars ended because a need for Indian allies was no longer essential.

From 1775 to 1791, Indian warriors won twenty-two battles such as the French Creek expedition. They were fearless fighters, and well-disciplined strategists. The European American armies made the mistake of thinking they were undisciplined, unknowledgeable "savages." Indian warriors became valued, but not completely trusted, and recruited to become allies for Euro-American armies as a part of expansion endeavors (Holms, 1996).

The Declaration of Independence ratified on July 4th, 1776, included provisions that involved the "merciless Indian Savages." While some Indian warriors exhibited extreme and harsh behaviors, European American soldiers were far more brutal. They maimed women and children of all ages. Indian babies were thrown to dogs as food while they were still alive, in front of their mothers. At the same time these atrocities were occurring, the American government continued to take steps to address the "Indian problem" under the pretenses that Indians were solely at fault for all the problems the white settlers were facing.

Henry Knox, Secretary of War, contacted George Washington during the summer of 1789. Knox proposed to Washington that Indian policy needed further clarification and additional revisions. Indian policy was customarily under the Articles of Confederation. Knox proposed that Indian tribes be considered foreign nations. Under the Constitution, authorization was given to Congress to control all commerce with foreign nations, which caused even further alienation between the white interlopers and the Indian people (Ellis, 2007). They were considered foreign inhabitants in their own country of origin.

During the 1790s, the United States government faced four alternatives concerning Indian policy. These options included extermination; re-location of Indian tribes to small plots of land, while towns sprouted up around them; assimilation by transforming them into Christian farmers; or relocation to unsettled territories west of the Mississippi. President Thomas Jefferson supported assimilation as the only viable and humane process.

In 1793, Congress gave authorization to George Washington to provide tribes with domestic animals and farm tools. Congress sent agents to demonstrate how to use these tools. Policymakers were pessimistic about the possible outcomes of these acts of assimilation. They believed the Indian people would not accept the White American culture and its value system and plans were being put into place to quarantine them.

President Jefferson's plan encompassed the transfer of the tribal people from the southern states to northern states. Plantations were set up in the southern states and slaves were utilized to enhance prosperity for the white settlers by expanding the goods produced by the wealthy landowners. The land in the south was divided into territories with a plan to establish states in the future. The lands vacated in the south by the Indians would be sold to help pay for part of the cost of Louisiana, via the Louisiana purchase.

William Henry Harrison put into place an Indian Removal policy in 1809, because Indian people were thought to lack the capacity to live up to White American standards. He negotiated the treaty of Fort Wayne in 1809, which ceded the majority of land in Indiana and Illinois to the white settlers. Harrison was not going to let a few "wretched savages" get in his way of settling an area that had the potential to support a large civilized population. He backed up his convictions with a large military garrison. Harrison became the governor of the Northwest Territories and then was elevated to one of the highest honors when he was elected as the 9th president of the United States (Sugden, 1997).

Contrary to how Harrison despised the Indian people, he did recognize the power and respect held by the Shawnee leader, Tecumseh. He gave careful consideration to this fearless leader. Harrison paid this tribute to Tecumseh:

"The implicit obedience and respect which the followers of Tecumseh pay to him is really astonishing, and more than any other circumstance bespeaks him on those uncommon geniuses, which spring up occasionally to produce revolutions and overturn the established order of things. If it were not for the vicinity of the United States, he would, perhaps, be the founder of an empire that would rival in glory that of Mexico or Peru. No difficulties deter him. His activity and industry supply the want of letters. For four years he has been in constant motion. You see him today on the Wabash and in a short time you hear of him on the shores of Lake Erie or Michigan, or on the banks of the Mississippi, and wherever he goes he makes an impression favorable to his purposes" (Sugden, 1997, p 215). Harrison defeated Tecumseh at the Thames River in 1813.

The U.S. government continued to find ways to address the "Indian Problem." Congress passed a bill in 1819 to establish a "civilization fund," which allotted ten thousand dollars for agricultural and literacy instruction of the Indian people. Missionaries provided assistance to those who were in agreement with participating in this program. These missionaries served dual roles. First and foremost, they wanted to Christianize the Indian people. Second, they provided instruction to them about the proper customs required to obtain citizenship. Missionary-sponsored farms and households were popping up in various locations in the country. These served as models of acceptable values and customs for Indian people to copy (Nies, 1996).

During the 1820s, Henry Schoolcraft visited the Ojibwe tribes and traveled with some Indian men. He was impressed with the wisdom of the tribal people and the detailed pictographs left behind by them at each area visited. The Secretary of War, John C. Calhoun, recommended Schoolcraft to the Michigan Territorial Governor, Lewis Cass, to assist with an expedition. The mission was to explore the land surrounding Lake Superior. Schoolcraft served as a geologist on the expedition.

Beginning in 1822, Schoolcraft conducted ethnological research while he was appointed the Indian agent at Sault Ste. Marie, Michigan. He learned the Ojibwe language from his wife, Jane Johnston, who happened to be of Ojibwe and Scottish/Irish descent. Schoolcraft's admiration for the native people quickly dissipated once he discovered that it would be more profitable to support the actions of Andrew Jackson. He took steps to obliterate the very same people who were connected to part of his wife's family, the Ojibwe people. One of the ways he did so was to take a portion of their written works and rewrite them to erase some of the Indian history. Schoolcraft also had a strong desire to obtain fame for his own written works. He went on to implement the Treaty of Washington in 1836, which took a large portion of land away from the Ojibwe and Odawa people (Bremer, 1987).

In support of President Jackson's efforts, Henry Schoolcraft resolved disputes over land with the Ojibwe and Odawa tribes. He employed tribal leadership to bring about the 1836 Treaty of Washington. The aforementioned tribes surrendered to the United States government a considerable amount of land worth millions of dollars. Schoolcraft believed these native people would be better off learning how to farm. Government officials established a subsidy system through which they were given supplies during the transition period from hunting to farming (Nobokov, 1992).

Treaties with the Indian people were negotiated by the President of the United States and were binding when approved by the Indians and two-thirds of the U.S. Senate. Many tribal people felt they had no choice but to give in to the U.S. government. The subjects dealt with in the treaties covered a variety of topics. The greatest number of treaties, 260 to be exact, were arranged between 1815 and 1860, during the prominent westward expansion. Almost 100 treaties specifically addressed land boundaries between a tribe and the United States. Two tribes, the Potawatomi and Chippewa in Michigan, negotiated forty-two treaties for each of their tribes, which was more than any other tribes. Not all of the 550 federally recognized tribes established treaties with the federal government (Utter, 1993). One of the most destructive treaties carried out in Michigan was the 1836 Treaty of Washington which was signed by leaders of the Chippewa and Odawa tribes. Approximately fourteen million acres of their land was taken from them.

"Article Six of the Constitution declares treaties to be the supreme law of the land, so treaties are just as valid today as they were on the day they were signed, and treaty rights are legally binding as well... The treaty rights are rights retained in treaties negotiated between sovereigns, and Native American tribes are recognized as sovereign nations. Treaty rights are tribal, not individual rights, and are held and regulated by the treaty signatory tribes. That interpretation of sovereign nation status later permitted Native American tribes to prevail in the adoption of gaming and casinos on their lands as an economic tool, which withstood court challenges" (Brody, 2019, paras. 54 – 55).

"The treaty rights, which include the right to hunt, fish and gather on established reservation land and certain other ceded territory, were reserved to specific tribes. These rights have been granted in perpetuity in exchange for the vast amount of land ceded to the federal government by Native American tribes—although they assert, they continually have to battle to enforce those rights" (Brody, 2019, para. 52).

By the 1840s, the American boundary reached the Pacific Ocean. Indian people were considered to be of heathen nature since they did not farm the land they lived on. Reservations served as a dumping ground for them. The population of these unfortunate people was numbered at only a few hundred thousand, reduced from millions when the Europeans first set foot in the Western Hemisphere (Ellis, 2007).

The mid 1840s was a turning point concerning the ideals of expansionism in the United States. Seeds were planted to adopt the principles of expansionism by John Adams and John C. Calhoun during the development of the original Constitution after the war of 1812, and further propagated by John L. O'Sullivan. O'Sullivan formally proposed the phrase "Manifest Destiny." "Manifest Destiny" involved the expansion of United States territory, which was considered prearranged by the Divine, and European immigrants were to be the beneficiaries. These beliefs further justified the takeovers of Indian resources, such as water, land, timber, silver, gold and other valuables. The expansion included a massive move westward to form a larger civilized land base for those who participated in the acts of freedom described by the federal government.

"Manifest Destiny" made its public debut in the *Democratic Review* in the July and August 1845 issues. O'Sullivan founded the *Democratic Review* and was a co-founder of the *New York Morning News*. During this time period, he was considered a scholar, visionary, as well as a politician, adventurer, and literary artist. With popularity on his side, the concept he advocated took hold of the American public like a storm.

The indigenous were forced, often through acts of heinous violence, to reside on reservations, which were plots of land chosen by outsiders. The passage of the Indian Appropriations Act of 1851 authorized the establishment of these reservations in the U.S. Often the land was not suitable for agriculture. Native American homelands were rich in natural resources such as sources of water, wild game and land that was suitable for agriculture, which enabled the people to provide for their families and communities. Approximately three hundred Indian Reservations were located in the United States. Today, there are five Indian Reservations located in Michigan.

Reservations ended up being a breeding ground for many of society's ills such as higher levels of suicide, poverty, substance abuse, domestic violence, and child abuse and neglect than the rest of the population. Groups of individuals, inflicted with historical trauma due to the genocide, and discrimination tactics of the Europeans since they first came to North America, resided together on small plots of land. Alcohol, introduced during the fur trading days, has led to many Native Americans' reliance to deaden their pain. A multitude of Native Americans today continue to suffer from historical trauma. The cumulative effects of chronic stress and unresolved historical trauma have led to an increased risk for developing psychological and behavioral disorders.

When the boarding school era began, Congress passed the General Allotment Act, also known as the Dawes Act, because Henry Dawes was its chief supporter. President Grover Cleveland signed this act. The General Allotment Act afforded the President the ability to distribute quarter sections (160 acres) of Indian reservation lands to each Indian person who was the head of a household. Bachelors over eighteen years of age received an eighth section. Those who accepted these allotments were required to live on their homesteads away from their fellow tribesmen. Another advantage to this initiative was to extend citizenship to the Native Americans as legal landowners. Therefore, Indian land could be and was taxed (Nies, 1996).

The Dawes Act was strongly enforced in Michigan. Any reservation land that was not appropriated to Indian people went to the Anglo invaders. The Dawes Act was a part of the assimilation process, which involved detribalization that caused Indian people to lose their tribal identities, and thus become American citizens. The "Indian problem" would fade away because Indian people would disappear into the fabric of American society and be a part of the large tapestry. The allotment process, which lasted two decades, caused long-lasting dependency and resentment by Indians and served as a catalyst for the accomplishment of the goals set forth by "Manifest Destiny."

The Indian Education Act of 1891 gave authority to government officials to control the location, activities and treatment of all Indian children and mandated the collection and transportation of tribal children to Indian boarding schools. Total control of Indian children's education was viewed as the most feasible option to achieve assimilation and the adaptation of a perceived "civilized" lifestyle for Native Americans. Some Indian people managed to survive with little to no repercussions after attending these institutions, however, for the majority of them, the boarding school initiative made a worse impact than all other efforts to destroy Indian people, which included massacres, starvation, disease, loss of land, and Christianity. The negative impact of the enforced boarding school legislation has resonated with many Native American families today. A multitude of them suffer from psychological problems stemming from historical trauma such as Post Traumatic Stress Disorder.

The introduction of the term "Manifest Destiny" supported the white settler belief that they had the divine right and privilege to pursue the takeover of all land and resources between the Atlantic and Pacific Oceans, or what is known today as the United States. Their beliefs were supported by the federal government, U.S. military, and by Roman Catholic Popes. As a result, tribal people throughout the United States have had to work diligently to rebuild their tribal governments and begin to regain a sense of balance after they have been victimized over and over by acts of discrimination, assimilation, and genocide. In spite of the social welfare programs put into place to address the problems Indian people have been facing, many still experience the social ills of domestic violence, substance abuse, child abuse, and neglect more than any other segment of the population. Land represented life, granted to the Native Americans by the Creator, to provide food and a place to live.

The beginning of the Europeans' financial endeavors started with the fur trade. Alcohol, which ruined the lives of many Native Americans since the fur trading days, was introduced as a cheap commodity in exchange for beaver pelts. Disease killed countless native people who did not possess immunity to its lethal properties. Sir Jeffery Amherst, a British officer, had a hand in killing thousands of Odawa people by intentionally exposing them to smallpox. Many foreigners believed it would behoove the native people to pick up a hoe and farm while they embraced Christianity. Indian children, forced to attend boarding schools, experienced many abuses. Reservations were filled with heartache and despair. Many Indian people, forced to succumb to oppression and discrimination, managed to survive, but not unscathed. The education and land policies were put into place to undermine their culture by uprooting them from their homes and enforcing a disciplined education and religion, along with a coerced hatred of their Indian heritage (Sharpes, 1979).

The History of Indian Boarding Schools

Steadfast Resiliency

The halls whisper the horrors
experienced by the victims.
Sexual, spiritual, emotional, and physical infliction.
Held hostage by boarding school legislation.
What happened to the children's souls?

Inadequate amounts of food, long spoiled.
Days spent in arduous labor,
washing floors, tending livestock and crops.

> Young minds coerced to believe
> they are savages, heathens, less than human.
> Homesickness, many children lost to illness,
> these places associated with death,
> Indian boarding schools.
>
> Parents in despair on reservations,
> while their children parish.
> Censored silence, untold truths.
> Demonstration of love forbidden.
> Children building strong alliances,
> through acts of camaraderie.
> Survival through steadfast resiliency.
> -By Sharon Brunner

The outcome of the boarding school legislation was a vulnerable population laced with disease, death, poverty, and other social ills, such as rates of domestic violence, alcoholism, child abuse and neglect higher than any other sectors of the population. Ongoing cultural oppression, health disparities, and a lack of access to services and economic opportunity coupled with chronic poverty, depleted hope for many tribal families. The cumulative effects of chronic stress and unresolved historical trauma led to an increased risk for developing psychological and behavioral disorders. The negative impact of the enforced boarding school legislation has resonated with many Native American families today.

"The way they went about it was horrific. They would just go to a town and round up the children… They would chop the Indian hair off, and in the Indian culture, hair is sacred. To make sure children wouldn't escape, they would tell them their parents died. We're a very spiritual people. When the children tried to do death rites, they were prohibited to pray or speak their language and they were punished for it. Many of the children were discombobulated, and horribly damaged." (Brody, 2019, para. 68).

"The truth about the US Indian boarding school policy has largely been written out of the history books. There were more than 350 government-funded, and often church-run, Indian Boarding Schools across the U.S. in the 19th and 20th centuries. Indian children were forcibly abducted by government agents, sent to schools hundreds of miles away, and beaten, starved, or otherwise abused when they spoke their native languages. Between 1869 and the 1960s, it's likely that hundreds of thousands of Native American children were removed from their homes and families and placed in boarding schools operated by the federal government and the churches. Though we don't know how many children were taken in total, by 1900 there were 20,000 children in Indian boarding schools, and by 1925 that number had more than tripled. The U.S. Native children that were voluntarily or forcibly removed from their homes, families, and communities during this time were taken to schools far away... Many children never returned home and their fates have yet to be accounted for by the U.S. government." (The National Native American Boarding School Healing Coalition, N.D., para. 3).

In Michigan, three boarding schools contained many children who were coerced or forced to attend during their time of operation. In 1860, the old St. Joseph Orphanage and School was built on the Assinins complex in the Upper Peninsula of Michigan about 500 acres north of the town of Baraga. It was built by Bishop Frederic Baraga, and although an orphanage, the core mission was "white assimilation and religious conversion." At a later date, it served as a boarding school for Native American children with the same core mission. The Holy Childhood Boarding School in Harbor Springs, Michigan opened in 1839 until 1884 when funding ran out, and then reopened in 1886 until 1983 and was church-run during its entire operation. The Federal Boarding School in Mt. Pleasant, Michigan opened on January 3, 1893 and closed in 1933. The federal government turned over the education of the Indian children to the state.

During the time the boarding schools were first established, families were forced to rely on the U.S. government for sustenance. They faced the threat of losing their much-needed rations, annuities and other goods if they did not let the government take their children and place them in these cold and harsh institutions. A compulsory attendance law was passed by Congress in 1891. As a result of the poor economy, many parents felt they had no choice but to send their children to the institutions because they could not provide for them (Child, 2000). Some of the children were provided better care when they attended the boarding schools because of the problems their parents faced, such as alcoholism. Other reasons why they attended the boarding schools included racism, which was endemic toward

Native Americans at the public schools, or they had cousins, siblings and other people they knew who attended the schools.

The concept of the boarding school initiative began in 1875 when Richard Henry Pratt was given responsibility of 72 Indian men charged with murder and rapine (the act of seizing property by force) at Fort Marion in St. Augustine, Florida. During their stay, these prisoners served as laborers to offset the cost of running the prison. They performed cleaning and maintenance duties. Pratt rehabilitated these men. The prisoners were introduced to reading and arithmetic in a classroom setting and worked part time at odd jobs at St. Augustine. The Indian men adopted the appearance and characteristics of the American population. These same Indian men were later placed in jobs without guards. Following Pratt's efforts to rehabilitate the Indian men, the Carlisle Indian Boarding School was established by Pratt in Carlisle, Pennsylvania with support of the federal government in 1879. The boarding schools were fashioned after the same rehabilitative principles as the prison program, which included the school attendants serving as laborers to offset costs (Child, 2000).

"A great general has said that the only good Indian is a dead one, and that high sanction of his destruction has been an enormous factor in promoting Indian massacres. In a sense, I agree with the sentiment, but only in this: that all the Indians there is in the race should be dead. Kill the Indian in him, and save the man." (General Richard Henry Pratt)

Native American children from various tribes and a multitude of locations from around the country were kidnapped from reservations where they were sequestered with their families by the U.S. government. School employees transported the children to the school where they succumbed to abuse and stripped of any semblance of their culture and self-respect, completely traumatized. As mentioned earlier, their hair was chopped off. (Their long hair represented their connection to Mother Earth, growth of their spirit, extrasensory perception and connection to all things.) School employees scrubbed them with kerosene and they were forbidden to use their native language, only English. They had to wear foreign clothing. In the effort to reform non-dominant cultures, they inflicted irreversible damage (Irving, 2014). By 1917, the final year of operation of the Carlisle Boarding School, there were 58 tribes represented in the student body (Child, 2000).

Girls dormitory at Mt. Pleasant Indian Industrial Boarding School (Clarke Historical Library and CMU, undated)

"The Carlisle school developed a "placing out system," placing Indian students in the mainstream community for summer, or a year at a time where they could learn skills other than farming. While monitored carefully at Carlisle, other outing programs were often exploitive. At the Phoenix Indian School, girls became the major source of domestic labor for white families, boys were placed in seasonal harvest or other jobs unwanted by white or immigrant laborers, and the students were unsupervised, learning very little from their outing experiences" (American Indian Relief Council, N.D., para. 11). Other boarding schools followed suit and many Indian children became laborers for white people who lived near the schools.

Children were given meaningless English names at the schools. In the Native American tribal way of life, one was not permitted to own anything that was provided to them by the Creator. The land, food and other necessities were bestowed to them to use and had to be honored. The only thing that could be owned was their given names. Only one person in a village had a specific name, and this name was derived by spiritual means such as visions, dreams and naming ceremonies. Names provided their identity throughout their lifetime. When English names were given to the children as a part of the assimilation process, this led to identity confusion." (Reyner and Eder, 2004).

"Conversion to Christianity was also deemed essential to the cause. Indian boarding schools were expected to develop a curriculum of religious instruction, placing emphasis on the Ten Commandments, the Beatitudes and Psalms. Implanting ideas of sin and a sense of guilt were part of Sunday schools. Christianity governed gender relations at the schools and most schools invested their energy in keeping the sexes apart, in some cases endangering the lives of the students by locking girls in their dormitories at night—meaning they could not get out, even in the case of fire..." (American Indian Relief Council, N.D., para. 14).

Religious instruction added to the confusion and degradation of many Indian children. Oftentimes, they were abused in various ways by the same people who were providing religious instruction. Children who demonstrated resistance to the teaching practices and the regimented authority were subjected to humiliation and harsh punishments. They suffered whippings and unusual torture such as standing on their tiptoes with arms outstretched while their hands were hit with wooden boards and rulers. The treatment of boys was typically more severe than that of girls. Ruthless punishment occurred when children tried to run away, although this did not deter many from attempting to do so.

It may be difficult to imagine the shock these children experienced when they were yanked from their homes and families, stripped of their cultural identity, while being forced to attend a foreign environment filled with fear and hostility. A strange form of religion was forced upon them while told they were savages. However, the dominant population continued to see a solid purpose for the establishment of these institutions. The Carlisle School led to the establishment of many similar boarding schools in various locations around the country with the intention of civilizing the Native American children to prepare them to fit into American society as servants and laborers. The transformation included vast changes in family structure, economics (how they earned a living), how they expressed emotion, and so much more (Irving, 2014). Their loss of identity formed mixed messages about their heritage and about themselves, resulting in contempt for those in power as well as their parents and elders.

Boarding schools resembled military camps. Indian children were stringently taught how to follow orders. The children had to fall into formation, march in a straight line, and oftentimes wore military clothing and shoes. During the weekdays, they attended educational sessions. They were taught English, math, history, and geography usually by American teachers. Geography was an eye-opening experience when they learned about the world and stars. When asked to draw pictures of the earth, they drew pictures of dwellings, animals and vegetation (Adams, 1995). Some of the teachers tried to be kind and helpful, but many were cruel and harsh.

On average, only a few hours a day was spent in the classroom, and the rest of the day was spent undertaking assigned tasks. The children received minimal care and education. Learning how to accomplish various tasks was thought to help prepare them for adulthood in the white man's world, because the only viable future was a white future. Girls were trained to work as servants or to become homemakers. Boys were trained in the areas of gardening, repair and maintenance of homes and farms, the running of farms, printing presses, and the building of houses and furniture.

The children suffered from various types of abuse, which included sexual abuse. One woman reported she spent years in therapy until she finally grasped the fact that she had been a victim. The shame and guilt she experienced as a result of the sexual abuse she was forced to endure at the hands of a priest at a missionary boarding school caused her chronic emotional stress into adulthood.

According to one report, nuns at the Holy Childhood Boarding School in Harbor Springs, Michigan maintained relationships with young boys and these young boys would become confidants for these women. Mentally healthy women in their 30s or 40s do not fall in love with boys who are 10, 11 or 12 years of age. Pedophiles work in a way that does not permit children to refuse. They were cunning, measured, and acted under the pretext of fondness. These children were used as sexual outlets. Once the sexually deviant person tired of their current victim, they dumped them and preyed on other unsuspecting children. Victims often felt abandoned. Children could not escape from their perpetrators. They had no one to turn to and they were held captive because these institutions became their prison (Stanton, 2008).

Another report involved nuns at the same boarding school who began their seduction by kissing the younger boys good night. One of the abusive nuns was in her 20s, rather plain and chubby. The favored boys would get kissed on the lips and she would tickle them. One of the people who attended the school stated that a few years went by for him until the kisses started getting longer and longer, and then he was taken to her bedroom. The boys were not expected to perform sexual acts until they were approximately 12 years of age.

One day, another nun at another institution pulled a boy off the playground and forced him to perform sexual acts. He and the pedophile nun were caught in a compromising position by other nuns, yet the perpetrator did not receive any retribution. The children were habitually exposed to "institutionalized pedophilia" and "sexual terrorism." The pedophiles included, but were not limited to, priests, nuns, teaching staff, and Protestant clergy (Podles, 2008).

When children first arrived at the school, they felt lonely and isolated and as a result many suffered from homesickness. Most children who attended these institutions were separated from their family before they were developmentally mature. The boarding schools were often one hour or further from the children's homes. The expense of travel, more than most Indian families could afford, deterred them from visiting their children. In 1924, the Native American per capita annual income was approximately $81 (Churchhill, 2004).

Prior to the 1920s, boarding school officials would have to seek preapproval from the local reservation superintendent or an Indian agent before permission could be granted for children to go home, even for severe hardship, such as deaths in the family and sick relatives. Indian parents learned to get around these sanctions by stating their children were needed to assist with farming. Since farming was a part of the assimilation process, it served as a more worthy excuse. When John Collier filled the position as Commissioner of Indian Affairs in 1933, these policies took a turn for the better. Students were permitted to go home for the summer months and usually for family hardships.

Indian children developed alliances with each other and looked after one another in school. Many of them had never met Indian people from other tribes. Long-lasting friendships were often formed, some lifelong. They made fun of the teachers and gave them names the students felt best suited their personalities. On occasion, they snuck out at night together and did forbidden activities, such as breaking into buildings on and off school property. Sports, choirs, bands, and dances were other ways long-lasting friendships were developed and ways in which the children maintained their sanity. Sharing the common experience of attending boarding schools was another way in which lifelong bonds were established.

When a child was sent to bed without a meal, the other children would often sneak them food. The children experienced what could be referred to as slow, agonizing starvation. School officials were allotted very limited funding, which served as a strong indication of the lack of importance concerning Indian children.

Because many Indian children from various tribal nations attended the boarding schools together, they shared a rich cultural exchange referred to as pan-Indianness. They developed an understanding of other Indian cultures while helping each of their acquired acquaintances with the harshness of the boarding school experience. Ojibwe students, for example, met Indian children from various tribes such as the Lakotas, Oneidas and Poncas from various locations around the U.S. They became more alike, learned a portion of other Indian languages along with the enforced English language. Students who left the boarding schools after graduation married people from other tribes and summer gatherings on reservations became intertribal events. New political alliances were created and the schools became a part of a joint history (Child, 2000).

The boarding school experiment proved to be successful concerning what the European Americans wanted to accomplish, which was to remove any semblance of being a Native American from the Indian children. The children could not speak their language and were told on a continuous basis their past way of life was barbaric. In order to save their souls, they needed to banish all Native American practices. Many of the children spent years at the boarding schools and when they returned to their families, they were treated as strangers. They didn't fit in with their families and their communities. In the effort to belong somewhere, they turned their lives over to drugs and alcohol and many of the young women became mothers without preparation for that role. They were not taught how to be parents at the boarding schools. As a result of the boarding school experience, many Native Americans still suffer from high rates of domestic violence, drug and alcohol abuse, child abuse and neglect and suicide.

Mt. Pleasant Boarding School

Historical Background

Originally, a day school, this institution was located in Mt. Pleasant, Michigan for Native American students. The school opened on January 3, 1893. By 1911, eleven red brick buildings were erected which included boys' and girls' dormitories, an assembly hall, dining room, hospital, powerhouse, laundry, storehouse, industrial building, and teachers' club. The staff at the hospital served the residents and staff of the school as well as the local residents. The education provided at this site was similar to that of other boarding schools during that time period. Thousands of Native American children from Michigan attended this institution. After graduating from the Mt. Pleasant boarding school, students either went on to finish their schooling at public high schools or were transferred to other federally run boarding schools such as Carlisle (Littlefield, 1983).

One half of the day was spent in the classroom and during the other half, the children had to provide for the upkeep of the school. The goal behind the chores involved preparation for adulthood and to provide maintenance of the school and its basic operations. The school operated in a military fashion with marching and the expectation of stringent obedience. Disobedience, tardiness, and other infractions were punished. Punishment included denial of privileges, extra work duties, and occasionally beatings with a strap or rubber hose. Children sometimes ran away, but it was reported that this was mainly due to their loneliness for family, not due to harsh treatment (Littlefield, 1996).

The staff placed a strong emphasis on agricultural instruction. The school was located on 200 acres, which was soon increased to 360 acres. Children learned how to grow a variety of fruits and vegetables and how to raise typical farm animals such as chickens and pigs. Their hope involved boys owning farms when they were adults so they could provide sufficiently for their families. Boys were also given training in various vocational areas such as tailoring, barbering, and carpentry (Littlefield, 1996).

Students at the Mount Pleasant Indian Industrial Boarding School (circa 1910)

Girls were trained to become domestic engineers or housekeepers. They learned how to do laundry without utilizing modern equipment, because they were likely to return to primitive settings. They were encouraged to do the employees' laundry at the school in order to earn money, and at the same time hone a necessary skill. The school provided them training in the areas of sewing, cooking, cleaning, and other domestic duties as deemed necessary (Littlefield, 1996).

In the heart of domination and inequality, the children demonstrated acts of resistance that we would be hard pressed to ignore. The significance of this resistance served as an indication of the strength and endurance of Native American people in general. In spite of the imbalance of power, these children found and maintained forms of solace through the interdependent interactions with their peers. Children made a game out of stealing food for themselves and their peers. They sneaked into the woods and make forts and went hunting much like their ancestors did. Some of the boys fished in the nearby ponds and rivers (Littlefield, 1989).

The twentieth century educational system evolved into a tool to promote and maintain the European American culture; a capitalistic society. All students were taught that obedience, punctuality, and maintaining control of emotions demonstrated respect. The latent reason behind the boarding school experience was the production of a working class, which continued to benefit those in power (Littlefield, 1989).

The curriculum and other practices matched that of other federally run schools. Basic academic subjects and vocational subjects were taught (Littlefield, 1983). The school provided up to eight years of instruction, later expanded to nine years (Littlefield, 1996). The school was closed due to federal budget cuts in 1933. The state was requested to accept the students into its school systems. The land, buildings and equipment were turned over to the state as a part of what was known as the Comstock Agreement. Part of the agreement took educational responsibilities concerning the special needs of Native American children from the federal government and placed the responsibility on the state of Michigan (VanAlstine, 1994). The closing of this school was a highly controversial matter. The state of Michigan utilized the property as a home for the mentally retarded after it was closed as an Indian boarding school (Littlefield, 1983).

Holy Childhood School in Harbor Springs

Historical Background

Members of the Odawa tribe in northern Michigan sent a request to Congress in 1823. They stated a need for a "teacher or minister of the Gospel." Their request was not met until 1829. At that time, Father DeJean settled in the L'Arbre Croche community better known today as Harbor Springs. A fifty-four by thirty-foot church with a school attached was erected at the site of the current Holy Childhood church. The school was in operation from 1839 to 1884, and closed because of a lack of funding. The Franciscan Fathers of Sacred Heart of St. Louis reopened the school. In 1886, the School Sisters of Notre Dame took over the administration of the school. In 1926, the present brick school was constructed. During the spring of 1983, the boarding school closed. In 1988, the day school closed and a day care center opened in its place (Elizalde, et al., 2015).

The purpose of this school was considered by the clergy to be a noble one. Native American children were provided housing, food, and education, and at the same time their souls were saved. Children were taught and supervised twenty-four hours a day. They were sent for various reasons, the two main ones being poverty and alcoholism. Because of the already existing generations of assimilation, parents and grandparents had been conditioned to believe they were less than

Holy Childhood of Jesus Indian School (Archives of Michigan, undated).

human, and thus needed to turn over their lives and the lives of their children to the European Americans (Elizalde, et al., 2015).

Unfortunately, the experience at the Holy Childhood Boarding School was not as positive for the attendants as it was for the students who attended the Mt. Pleasant Boarding School. Students were told that they had to embrace Christianity or they would burn in hell. The threat of beatings and public humiliation served as some of the ways the nuns maintained order and obedience.

This boarding school ended up being a place where students discovered that skin color did make a difference in regard to treatment (Elizalde, et al., 2015).

The staff assigned numbers to the children, which were attached to their clothing, toothbrushes, and beds. The numbers represented the regimentation of their lives. A strict schedule consisted of prayer, school,

chores, meals, play and television or movie times (Kolker and Golder, 1994).

One of the most disturbing factors was the rate of sexual abuse. According to Kolker and Golder (1994), this was not linked to the priests that were assigned there. The nuns were associated with this abuse. Reading further revealed that both men and women were interviewed, who attended the Holy Childhood boarding school. Of the eighty men and women, nine former male students stated they were sexually abused. The abuse occurred repeatedly and they expressed they felt there was no choice but to comply with the abuse. Otherwise, they feared the sanctions would have been unbearable (Kolker and Golder, 1994).

Students at Holy Childhood were often referred to as "black savages" or "heathens." A former attendee said "Even a lot of people I know right today still don't believe in God because every time they [got] hit, beat or whatever, it was in the name of the Lord." Another statement was "By the time I got out of that school, I didn't want nothing" (Stanton, 2008).

However, there were some fond memories. Not all of the sisters were abusive. Some of them said consoling words and gave gentle encouragement. They were the ones who the children could turn to when they needed positive attention. There were different standards for discipline during the period of time the school was in operation. Corporal punishment was widely accepted. However, the philosophy behind the Holy Childhood boarding school appeared to differ from that of the Mt. Pleasant boarding school. The Mt. Pleasant philosophy appeared to utilize vocational and domestic training as their way to assimilation. The philosophy behind the Holy Childhood boarding school was based on religious training and humiliation. Both had the same goal in mind, to dominate, and to promote the values of the European Americans. Vast differences existed between the way children were taught traditionally by their parents before the onset of the boarding school phenomena and the way the Native American children were taught at the boarding schools.

Comparison of Teaching and Learning Practices

Education was put into place with two main goals in mind. The first was to provide information to an individual so that they gained a better understanding of who they were and how they fit into all the social circles life encompassed. Another important goal implied that the educational process involved preparation for adulthood. Training included practicing the necessary skills to enhance the development of children into productive citizens of their communities (Miller, 1996).

Native American approach to education placed importance on looking, listening, and learning. Children were encouraged to observe

Holy Childhood of Jesus Indian School (Harbor Springs Historical Society, undated)

adults with the implicit purpose to look, listen and learn. The adults participated in a number of methods for providing the pertinent lessons to their children. These included conditioning their behaviors by demonstrating positive examples in their homes and communities, the provision of subtle encouragement through games, and they relied heavily on oral traditions to instill important messages that would be carried out throughout their lives. The stories elders and other adults told the children relayed information about the creation of the world, its contents, and how the various individuals populated the world and where they stood in relation to one another. Proper behavior, implied by indirect and non-coercive means, was in contrast to European American childrearing practices, which reflected abuse and deprivation (Miller, 1996).

Language and values symbolized the strengths of the Native American culture and aided in the learning process about the environment. The spiritual balance of many Native American people has been threatened as the result of the educational system. Because of this, a multitude of Native Americans developed social and psychological problems while they struggled to understand and possibly maintain a true sense of their Native American identity (Fixico, 2000).

The patterns and methods in which Native American learned best was drawn from their cultural backgrounds. They preferred to work and learn in groups and did not want to be singled out even when it came to being asked questions. They feared ridicule. Children were often punished in front of their peers for not understanding their schoolwork at the boarding schools. They relied on the teachers' expertise to guide them through the learning process. Intently listening was considered a sign of respect and most Native American children were taught to be respectful to adults at all times (Fixico, 2000).

Native American children's brains function differently from their European American peers. They tend to be right-brain oriented, which is associated with art, music, and other forms of creativity. They also tend to be more interested in the abstract areas of thought. In contrast their European Americans tend to be left-brained, associated with the concrete sciences. Failure in the classroom led to feelings of inferiority as a result of their educational needs not being met and the lack of respect they were shown (Fixico, 2000).

Native American youth saw themselves as members of their community. The sole purpose of this membership was unity. The achievement of grades caused the Native American students to stand out in class, which they did not like. The European American culture promoted individual accomplishment, but, Native American people traditionally preferred not be distinguished from the rest of the family or community. Their culture reflected cooperation and was communal based, not competitive and individualistic (Fixico, 2000).

The twentieth century marked a period of change for the educational process for Native American students.

Abyss and Revitalization Period: (Twentieth Century):

Community

All affirmed the central role of Indian prophecy, the bond between Indians and "Mother Earth," the existence of sacred "powers" by which ritual specialists benefited their people. They agreed to restore spiritual practices, encourage native language use, and combat alcoholism and family disintegration.

Little Star, Tribe Unknown
American Indian

During the early 1900s, liberal government officials created a more tolerant atmosphere toward Native American culture. President Roosevelt's "New Deal" stirred hope for Native Americans concerning the renewal of their cultural traditions. However, before that, the Bureau of Indian Affairs (BIA) worked on coercing them to become peaceful farmers by buying into their white neighbors' morality and materialism. A BIA directive denounced the Sun Dance and other spiritual ceremonies. Idleness and superstitions have been linked to these ceremonies (Bowden, 1981). The Twentieth Century represented vast changes from the termination era to ways in which Native American families were protected by the implementation of the Indian Child Welfare Act.

In 1924, Congress implemented the "Citizen Act." Native Americans became citizens of their own country. During the next three decades, the BIA continued to break up parcels of communally held land and allot it to individual families. European American businessmen took advantage of unsuspecting Native Americans and leased or bought approximately two million acres per year held in trust for Native Americans (Bowden, 1981).

By 1928, most Native Americans lived in poverty. That same year, Lewis Meriam conducted a historical study. His report indicated the vast majority of Native Americans suffered from a lack of health care and educational opportunities (see Appendix 6). The European American economic and social standards were of no of benefit to them. The "Great Depression" served as a more imposing hardship than it did to most of the other U.S. citizens. Policy makers continued to ignore the needs of tribal people even after the Meriam report was publicized (Bowden, 1981).

Michigan governmental officials were given the responsibility to undertake and meet the obligations set forth by the federal government, which included the practical and financial obligations the federal government owed the Native American people in the state of Michigan. For approximately thirty years, the state government did little to assume the responsibilities the Comstock agreement transferred to it (Clarke Historical Library, 2001). This period of educational neglect was referred to as the abyss period.

The Johnson O'Malley Act of 1934 was put into place to address education, medical attention, agricultural assistance, and social welfare. The Act included provisions for the Secretary of the Interior to develop separate contracts with a state or territory. The Johnson O'Malley Program funds were not made available to Michigan Native American children until 1971 (VanAlstine, 1994).

In 1936, the Act was amended to include provisions that extended to public and private institutions, corporations, agencies, and political subdivisions of the state or territory. The act in regard to education was meant to address the special educational needs of Native American children (Strickland, 1982).

The same year the Johnson O'Malley Act was introduced, the Indian Reorganization Act (IRA) was also implemented. President Franklin Roosevelt appointed John Collier as the Commissioner of Indian Affairs. He was an active participant of the reform movement and many of his proposed philosophies were a part of this policy. The goal of this act was to revitalize tribal organizations and tribal community life. The long-range policy leaning toward assimilation still remained the same (Strickland, 1982).

During the late 1940s, the government decided to continue to coerce the tribal people from their lands and communities for various reasons. One reason was the costs allotted to provide financial support them. Another was the clearing of reservations for purposes of mining. The overarching reason was to continue the process of assimilation.

In spite of these acts of discrimination, Indian men continued to "fight the white man's wars." "According to John Collier, then Commissioner of Indian Affairs, there were 7,500 American Indians in the armed forces as of June 1942, less than six months after the attack on Pearl Harbor. By October of that year, another observer reported that the number of Native Americans in the military had risen to well over 10,000. By 1944, almost 22,000, not counting those who had become officers. At the war's end, there were over 25,000 Native Americans scattered throughout the military services, with the bulk of them in the U.S. Army" (Holms, 1996, p 104).

Native Americans primarily fought in the American wars because they linked being a warrior with honor, and because they felt they were upholding what the Indian people promised in treaties; however, the American government did not honor treaty obligations.

In 1945, congressional opponents pursued endeavors to enforce assimilation of Native Americans to the white population's cultural practices. John Collier, who was forced to resign, emphasized cultural pluralism for American Indians. Their approach involved termination. Terminating Indian reservations, terminating all treaty obligations, and terminating all government programs that served Native Americans were some of the methods of the proposed enforced assimilation. Their culture was considered immaterial, anti-American and did not hold historical, cultural or legal ramifications for those who pursued the termination efforts.

Reservations were viewed as segregation and believed to have slowed the process of assimilation. They intended to dismantle the reservation system and utilize the natural resources located on specific reservations for private non-Indian companies, and to place the responsibility of Indian affairs on state and county governments. They wanted the federal government out of the Indian business. Termination policies ended the federally recognized status of approximately 100 tribal nations. State jurisdiction lorded over the affected tribes. Many Native Americans suffered cultural shock when they were forced to relocate to urban slums and other areas. The termination process weakened tribal governments and had a long-lasting, damaging effect on their civil liberties (Native American Partnership, 2013).

Beginning in 1952, federal policymakers passed legislation that allowed the storage of highly radioactive waste byproducts from the mining of uranium primarily in reservation areas. Mining was also conducted in reservation areas in spite of massive amounts of ore deposits located in other locations. Maximization of profits for energy corporations served as the motive for these mining practices. The Navajo, Lugunas and other tribal communities were exposed to highly carcinogenic and mutagenic agents as a result of these mining maneuvers. The storage of nuclear waste has continued to occur on reservations such as the Mescalero Apache Reservation in New Mexico, in the Yucca Mountain area, and the Navajo treaty land base (Churchhill, 1997).

In 1964, the Office of Economic Opportunity was established. It bestowed opportunities for Native American children and adults to participate in programs. A variety of programs were introduced such as Head Start, Upward Bound, Job Corps, Vista, and Indian Community Action Programs. The purpose of these initiatives was to help those in need rise to higher standards of living (VanAlstine, 1994).

In 1965, the Elementary and Secondary Act assisted disadvantaged youth both economically and socially. Titles I and II of the Act were extended to include BIA-administered schools. Following, there was a push to encourage more tribal and parental involvement in regard to the education of Native American youth (Van Alstine et al., 1994). As a method of holding onto part of their heritage such as communal life, Native Americans created social and political organizations. This occurred in the 1970s and 1980s. During the 1990s, intertribal activities began blossoming more. Native American organizations and gatherings formed the much-needed alliances and supported the growth of pan-Indianism. Socialization was the priority. Political issues were placed second in regard to goals (Fixico, 2000).

The American Indian Movement (AIM), created in Minneapolis, Minnesota in 1968, served as a means of protecting the rights of Indian people. This movement replaced an anti-poverty program based in Minneapolis. AIM was originally referred to as Concerned

Indian Americans, until members recognized the acronym to be that of the Central Intelligence Agency. The initial goals of AIM included the improvement of economic and educational conditions for Indian people.

Many Vietnam veterans returned to the United States and found an unbearable situation and became members of AIM. The majority of Indian people were still living in poverty. Vietnam veterans who experienced "cognitive dissonance" as a result of fighting in that war turned their psychological distress into political activism. The term "cognitive dissonance" refers to when people's values and beliefs turn out to be drastically different from the realities they are experiencing (Holms, 1996).

Again, many Indian men fought in wars because they felt they were upholding requirements set forth by treaties between their tribes and the U.S. government. "Why was I fighting to uphold a U.S. treaty commitment halfway around the world when the United States was violating its treaty commitments to my own people and about 300 other Indian nations? I was fighting the wrong people, pure and simple..." (Holms, 1996, page 175).

According to Indian activists, the government was continuing to instill policies associated with sadistic national colonialism. Native Americans were openly questioning termination, and relocation which resulted in extreme levels of poverty and other serious issues that has existed and continued to exist on reservations. AIM became a part of a crusade process that strove to restore treaty rights, and change the educational system. Under the educational system, Indian people were taught self-hatred, and the goal of AIM was to reestablish and safeguard tribal identity (Holms, 1996).

Congress passed the Indian Education Act in 1972. Provisions included the establishment of a supplemental entitlement program for Native American education in public schools and the creation of the National Advisory Council on Indian Education. In 1975, Congress passed the Indian Self-Determination and Educational Assistance Act, which consisted of the allocation of contracts for tribes for BIA educational programs and other BIA-operated programs. Following in 1978, standards were put into place for the running and administering of BIA schools (Van Alstine et al., 1994). (Refer to Appendix 2 for more information about the History of Federal Indian Education Policy.)

In 1972, Indian activists organized a massive march on Washington, D.C., known as the Trail of Broken Treaties. The caravan formed on the West Coast and wound its way across the nation, picking up followers as it went. It arrived in Washington during the final week of the presidential campaign. Native Americans poured into the city. The bulk of them assembled at the Bureau of Indian Affairs building to await word regarding where they were to be housed during their stay at the capital. Eventually they were told they were to be housed in the Department auditorium.

As they were leaving the BIA, guards began to push a number of people out the door. The young protesters turned on the guards and seized the building. The occupation of the BIA building lasted for nearly a week before the Indian people agreed to leave. In return, the federal government agreed not to prosecute the protesters (Holms, 1996). For many years, federal agents conducted secret missions to discredit and eventually put behind bars the entire leadership of the American Indian Movement. Today, AIM has continued to be an active advocate for Native American rights.

During the 1970s, an organization called the Indian Health Service (IHS) was established to provide services to Indian people, but implemented sterilization services for Indian women. This program resulted in involuntary and oftentimes uninformed sterilization of 42% of all Indian women of childbearing age, in an attempt to decrease the Indian population and as part of the genocide efforts. The sterilization program was ceased in 1976. During the same time period, approximately 13,000 Navajos residing in the Big Mountain region in Arizona were removed from this land base to make way for the Peabody Coal Company (Churchhill, 1997).

The Indian Child Welfare Act, passed by Congress on November 8, 1978 and signed by President Carter, was implemented after numerous hearings held with the Senate to cover all issues regarding the status of Native American people. The most significant discovery of these hearings was the high percentage of Native American families broken up by the removal of their children from them. A rate of twenty-five to thirty-five percent of all Native American children were removed from their homes (Goodluck, 1993).

The trend reflected self-determination for Indian tribes at the federal level. The U.S. Constitution and the federal government supported this. President Bill Clinton issued Executive Order 13084 on May 14, 1998, which was referred to as the "Consultation and Coordination with Indian Tribal Governments" (Mason, 1998). In Michigan, progress was made in the area of economic development. However, further steps needed to be taken to enhance economic growth. The Bureau of Indian Affairs addressed a more liberal funding policy for tribes and tribal entities to establish more entrepreneurial activities (Cleland, 1992).

Several national studies have included the study of Native American education from the past to the present. Among these are the Meriam Report; The National Study of American Indian Education; The Kennedy Report; and the American Indian Policy Review Commission. The constant concern described in these studies was Native American parents not given the opportunity to be involved in the governance of their children's education. The educational process has finally gone full circle. This period of time marked the revitalization for the education of Native American children. The Bureau of Indian Affairs recognized the need for changes in regard to their educational policies and accepted responsibility for the negative sanctions placed on Native American people (Champagne, 1994).

The Department of the Interior has given primary responsibility to the Bureau of Indian Affairs (BIA) for the administration of Native American programs. The BIA had under its command one hundred and eighty-five federally recognized tribal or Bureau managed schools (Mehojah, 2000). Congress took notice of the problems concerning the administration of BIA schools from the Bureau itself and has introduced amendments to address these issues. A public apology, issued by Kevin Gover, Head of the Federal Bureau of Indian Affairs, concerned the hardships caused by the insensitivity of the BIA officials toward the Native American population in the past (Sault Tribe News, 2000). (Refer to Appendix 3)

Another dilemma faced by many Native American people was the question: who is an Indian? A definition needed to be developed by the various tribal and governmental entities in order to make the determination about who will share the benefits of tribal people. Blood quantum issues created dissention amongst tribal people. To define Indianness had to include both predicated biological factors and a cultural sense and feeling of belonging to a distinct part of history. The idea of blood quantum was based on the quantitative approach from the early nineteenth century. The struggle to gain access to these privileges has been a long and difficult journey (Cleland, 1992).

The lifestyle of Native Americans promoted an interdependence on one another. The idea behind Pow wows, which still occur today, was not primarily a maintenance of culture, but one of socialization. The drum and the various dances revitalized one's cultural heritage. Sweat lodge ceremonies were and continue to be practiced within Native American communities. Many tribal entities continue to utilize herbs for medicinal and other spiritual practices. Communal gatherings and storytelling continue to be practiced today. Storytelling has always been an important method of providing instruction and entertainment for Native Americans of all ages (Fixico, 2000).

Involvement in traditional practices and the support of family and friends provides a source of strength for Native American people. To aid in the process of them joining together to practice their spiritual beliefs, The American Indian Religious Freedom Act of 1978 was passed. This act permitted them to exercise their traditional spiritual practices. They could use and possess sacred items and they obtained the right to worship through ceremonies and traditional rites. Their spiritual rights had been outlawed during the late 1800s.

The educational process for Native American children was developed differently than for others in the United States. Approximately four hundred treaties throughout history have included provisions for educational services. These treaties were put into place in conjunction with the federal government and the tribal nations. The treaties involved land exchanges, protection against invasions, and self-government in lieu of the provision of services. The Bureau of Indians Affairs was created because of the unique relationship between the federal government and the tribal entities. For approximately one hundred years, the educational system for Native Americans was operated with the goal of assimilation. Progress has been made to address the educational needs of the Native American children (Champagne, 1994).

Twenty-first Century: Establish a U.S. Truth and Healing Commission

The citizens of the U.S. have a right to know the truth about the injustices inflicted on Native Americans for over 150 years as the result of the Indian boarding school legislation. Tribal children were taken or coerced from their families and forced to attend government- and religious-run Indian boarding schools. The schools served as a tool for colonization, assimilation, and genocide, which resulted in a loss of their language, culture, traditional foods, and permanent disruption of many families. Survivors of these schools described incidents of physical, sexual, psychological, and spiritual abuse and neglect. Many of the children died, went missing, or were murdered at the hands of boarding school employees.

A Truth and Reconciliation Commission of Canada (TRC) was established, and this organization has brought to light the hardships inflicted upon many Canadian Indians as a result of the residential schools. Serious efforts have been made to locate and identify a multitude of the missing children who died at the residential schools. The Canadian government exhibited their remorse when they honored the survivors with a public apology, which has not occurred in the U.S. The Canadian commission created a legal settlement between the Residential Schools Survivors, the Assembly of First Nations, Inuit representatives and the institutions responsible for the creation and operation of the schools: the federal government and church entities.

Steps have been taken to address the long overdue actions to rectify the harm caused by the boarding school legislation in the U.S. A group referred to as the National Native American Boarding School Healing Coalition (NABS) has been working to pass a bill that would establish a Truth and Healing Commission concerning Indian Boarding School Policies in the U.S. Their mission: To lead in the pursuit of understanding and addressing the ongoing trauma created by U.S. Indian Boarding School Policies. The bill introduced by NABS called "Truth and Healing Commission on Indian Boarding School Policies Act" labeled S. 1723 – 118th Congress (2023-2024) went before the Senate on May 18th, 2023. In June 2023, the bill was amended and passed by the Senate Committee on Indian Affairs. S.

1723 is being prepared for a full Senate vote. On February 5, 2024, the House introduced the bill as H.R. 7227. The bill need to be passed by the House Committee on Natural Resources before being presented to the House for a full vote. (Refer to: boardingschoolhealing.org/truth commission to check on the progress of the federal government concerning the proposed act).

A lot of work needs to be accomplished to start rectifying the harm caused by the Indian boarding school legislation in the U.S. First of all, the U.S. government needs to formally acknowledge and apologize for the harm caused by the Indian boarding school legislation. To date, there have not been any records accounting for the number of tribal children who were forced to attend these institutions. the number of Native American children who were abused, died, or have been missing while at these schools, and the long-term impacts on Native children who were forced to attend the Indian boarding schools.

A federal commission is needed to address the lack of recorded data concerning the 521 known boarding schools in the U.S., of which 408 received funding from the federal government. In addition to the search and compilation of records, a commission would also bring together boarding school survivors with a union of tribal representatives and experts in education, health, and children and families to fully delineate and understand the impacts of the federal Indian boarding school legislation.

As what has been discovered in Canada, the truth will emerge about what has been buried on Indian boarding school grounds. How many bodies will be uncovered? A limited amount of time exists to gather and record the stories from the survivors. This book has made a start with a few survivors. A Congressional Commission will assist with ensuring that accounts of Indian boarding schools told by survivors, families and undisclosed records can be conserved. It is vital that the children who were forced to attend these schools won't be forgotten. The harm caused by the boarding school legislation needs to be acknowledged to enable future generations to understand the impact it has had on tribal people. Americans must know the truth, so that this never happens again. (The National Native American Boarding School Healing Coalition, N.D.)

As stated earlier, Native Americans suffered at the hands of the European invaders for many years. They lost their land, suffered from cultural disruption, loss of children as a result of the boarding school legislation, placed on reservations in which they had to rely on the government for their basic needs, and introduced to the harmful effects of alcohol during the fur trading days. The list can go on and on. Native Americans suffer higher rates of substance abuse and suicide than the rest of the population. It is high time the U.S. government steps up to the plate to address the unmet needs of the Native American population and fully recognize the harm caused by multiple legislative acts such as the boarding school legislation.

Chapter 3 – Methodology

An exploratory qualitative research design was used to gather data for this project. The problem described for this study was broad in nature. The kind of questions asked during the unstructured interviews were exploratory in nature and an attempt was made to gather facts and thoughts with an unmapped contextual base. (Refer to Appendix 5.) In essence, the research participants told their stories about their families of origin and about their boarding school experience in a manner in which they felt most comfortable. Each participant was asked broad and open-ended questions. This allowed for flexibility and thorough in-depth answers. This type of participatory research involved listening and envisioning the message the research participants tried to convey. The oral histories provided assistance with a developed understanding about their system of meanings in the context of which they were given (Saleebey, 1997).

In 2001, I chose to begin this project because of my personal family background and personal involvement with tribal entities. My mother attended one of the boarding schools covered by this project. I was determined to study the experiences of those who attended two boarding schools, the Federal Mt. Pleasant and Holy Childhood Boarding Schools. The plights, such as alcoholism, that Native American people have continued to face may be symptoms of their boarding school experience. My own family has been plagued with alcoholism among other serious problems.

Many of Native American families I have previously met have demonstrated various strengths and a sense of pride in being a Native American person. Other Native American people appeared to be struggling with issues with severe impact on their lives and the lives of their families. I wanted to explore these areas more thoroughly to determine what may be the possible aftereffects of the boarding school experience.

Native American people who attended these boarding schools were members of different tribes. These individuals resided in various areas throughout the state of Michigan. I wanted to have other tribes represented in this study and not only focus on tribal members from the Sault Ste. Marie Tribe of Chippewa Indians (Sault Tribe). The referral process, snowballing techniques and personal knowledge led to the selection of the interview participants. They in turn were asked to assist me with identifying other potential subjects. I personally knew a few of them.

Contacts were conducted in person and by phone, to individuals who worked for tribal entities within and outside of the Sault Tribe to seek information about other possible interview participants. I attended a workshop in Mt. Pleasant and met with an elder, who agreed to participate in the study. Some of the interview participants gave me names of persons to contact for possible interviews. The age and health of some of those who attended the Mt. Pleasant boarding school ruled out some of potential interviewees. The Mt. Pleasant boarding school was closed in 1933, so many of the people who attended the school were elderly or deceased by 2001, when the interviews were conducted. The process for selecting interview participants who attended the Holy Childhood boarding school was not affected by such a large time lag, because the school closed in 1983.

Interviewees participants chose the location for the interviews. The interviewing sessions went from one to four hours in duration. Participants were made aware of possible follow-up contact if more information was required. The sessions were audiotape recorded. I took notes when it was possible, and added dialogue to the interview when it was appropriate. Nine interviews were conducted, three with individuals who attended the Mt. Pleasant Boarding School. One lived in Haslett, Michigan, and two in Sault Ste. Marie. Six interviews were conducted with survivors of the Holy Childhood Boarding School in Harbor Springs, one from Sugar Island, one from Sault Ste. Marie, three from St. Ignace, and one from Petoskey. The interviews were held at the participants' homes with the exception of the one conducted in Petoskey, which was at the participant's place of employment. The participants were members of the Sault Tribe, or the Little Traverse Band of Odawa Indians. Each interview participant was given an "Informed Consent" form to read. Time was allotted for questions regarding the form, and before the interviews began, they were requested to complete and sign it before the interview could proceed. (Refer to Appendix 4) The participants were informed the interviews would be kept confidential and they would be given another name when the contents of the interview were utilized in the body of the master's thesis. The city name and what boarding school they attended would be the only identifiers.

The interviews began with the development of rapport between the interviewee and the interviewer. Tobacco was presented as a gift to most of the participants. I explained the interview process and the goals of the project. I informed the participant that she/he was a cultural guide, and expressed my own ignorance regarding the participants' experiences (Leigh, 1998). The interviews were held from April to June 2001. I transcribed the audiotape interviews in my home office. I summarized the interviews and themes drawn from the compiled data.

"Communicating for Cultural Competence," which included a self-evaluation form for ethnographic interviews, was used to self-monitor the interview process and as a reminder of what techniques work to the advantage of both the researcher and the interview participant (Leigh, 1998). I reviewed the self-evaluation form before and after each interview to reinforce and monitor my interview skills. I took mental notes about what skills I needed to improve for future interviews.

I conducted the analysis portion of this project in a systematic order. After the interviews were transcribed, they were thoroughly read. Next, I summarized the individual interviews and placed into them two categories. Each of the two boarding schools represented an individual category. The boarding schools became reference points to delineate any differences that may have occurred between the experiences of those who attended either institution. My personal background again came into play with this decision. My point of reference related to personal family history and how it was associated with the Holy Childhood boarding school. Additionally, I wanted to investigate the alternative to a missionary-run school. The data were separated by boarding schools to gain a better understanding of the experiences as it pertained to the specific boarding schools. Inductive reasoning served as the rationale for this decision.

The summaries were examined closely and themes derived from

each summary. The number of times a theme was represented in each summary was documented, and separated by each interview participant. The themes that were noted more than once for all of the summaries were listed on a handwritten table. Then the themes were dispersed into the time periods in which they occurred. For example, one person stated that his family suffered from poverty when he was a child. This aspect provided the rationale for why he was sent to the boarding school. The theme of poverty was placed under the section referred to as the epistemology of the family of origin in each individual interview participant's table where it occurred.

A summary of the results for each time period was completed and placed on the individual tables. Each table for the summary of results depicted the themes and a separation between responses for those who attended the two boarding schools, which exposed the differences and similarities between the two groups.

In order to determine the aftereffects and perseverance of Native American people, I had to make comparisons from their situations of growing up with their families of origin, their boarding school experience, and what their lives were like in the present. Every effort was made to disallow my personal bias to come into play when the results of this study were calculated and listed in the result section.

Horizontal and vertical analysis of the criteria obtained from this study was utilized to delineate the similarities and differences between the results as denoted by the three time periods. The vertical and horizontal information was portrayed by the use of tables, which symbolized the individual interviews covered horizontally the time periods and vertically the persons interviewed and the themes indicated by the analysis of the interview summaries. The titles of the tables represented the order in which the oral historical accounts were portrayed in this thesis, and the boarding school the interview participants attended. Again, the time periods covered the epistemology of the family of origin, the boarding school experience and the post-boarding school experience.

The compiled results from all of the individual interviews were summarized. The horizontal axis symbolized the boarding school in which the interview participants' attended and the major themes depicted in the interview summaries. The vertical axis located the major themes and the number of interview participants. Regarding the themes delineated by the individual interviews, each had to be represented more than once to be recognized in the vertical column.

The discussion portion compared the three time periods listed in the summary of results section. Theoretical perspectives were applied to assist me with a possible rationale for explaining the discovered phenomena. The discussion covered the themes delineated in the analysis of the raw data and separated into various formats to assist with making a determination as to the positive and negative impact of the boarding school experience.

A literature review was conducted throughout the entire project. The available literature did not adequately cover the experiences of the Holy Childhood boarding school students and boarders. Only brief statements and a brief summary in a few newspaper articles were found. Although these sources were useful, they were not comprehensive enough to provide a clear picture about the experience of those who attended these institutions. Many of the sources covered the federal boarding schools throughout the nation as a whole, and in Canada. Concerning the Mt. Pleasant boarding school, Dr. Alice Littlefield described the experience of some of the boarders. However, the available circulating materials did not cover information about their families of origin and their present lives.

Other studies and literature resources have covered the experiences of Native American people who attended the federal and missionary boarding schools, as I described in the previous chapter. (Refer to the bibliography) Experiences have not been examined of those individuals who have attended either the Mt. Pleasant or Holy Childhood boarding schools in the same study.

I have provided information about the three time periods of the boarding school boarders' lives and brought to the forefront some of the aftereffects of their boarding school experience. A project of this nature that compares experiences of two boarding schools has not been conducted to the my knowledge. Much has been learned about the aftereffects of the boarding school experience for the nine participants who attended these institutions through steps taken to analyze and decipher the data collected during this study.

Chapter 4 – Results

Oral Historical Accounts

All the interviews were transcribed, and summarized for the purpose of this project. The interview summaries were separated by the boarding schools attended. The Mt. Pleasant boarding school is reported first.

Mt. Pleasant Boarding School
Interview #1: Jeff from Haslett, Michigan

Jeff was born in Custer, Michigan in Mason County, approximately eighty years ago. His parents raised him on the reservation until he was five years old. For many Native American fathers, it was close to impossible to support their families on the reservation. Jeff's family moved to Muskegon and his father obtained employment at the rag and metal, a junk yard. The house they lived in according to Jeff was inadequate. *"We had substandard housing. The wind would come off the lake and just rattle those panes... They would just rattle. We had inadequate heat. I mean it was terrible... So I stayed there and then our family broke up, mostly due to alcohol... He would get his paycheck and would stop in the bars with his friends. There would be a lot of boozing it up. It broke up my family..."*

"The government expected the Indian to farm. They didn't know anything about farming. They'd try. They put the reserve on the poorest land. Nobody wanted it back in the early 1900s. It was timbered off and sand. But I remember my dad coming up the road with a big steelhead, the tail of the fish dragging in the sand... They were big fish... He hunted but hunting was poor. Game was scarce. But I remember we ate duck and a lot of wild game, venison and small rodents, squirrels I suppose. It's good eating... The social status of the Indians back in those days, they were unemployed,

uneducated, and actually it was some of the government's responsibility. Put them on a reserve that a wolf would starve to death on. Expected them to make a livelihood on that sand so they all drifted into the cities... Some of them were shipped out West. Some of them, they either couldn't collar them. I think in my case, my father... wasn't full blooded Indian... is one reason why our family wasn't shipped out West... my dad was Irish, too. I'm sure that's one reason why, like my aunt, they married white people in that area."

His mother had difficulty meeting the basic needs of her children because of the problems his father was having with alcohol. *"The probate court intervened... They shipped my three sisters and me to the Indian boarding school in Mt. Pleasant... I was six... We went to the Indian school, that was a plus... I finished the seventh grade, then the next year in 1933, they closed that school down. My sisters had finished the ninth grade... The object of the Indian school was for assimilation. With me it worked. This is the important thing. I was with white people all my life. My parents didn't have the wherewithal to maintain a family."*

The interview moved into a discussion about what the boarding school experience was like in his eyes. Jeff explained a regular day and what his training involved: *"When I first came there, I was lonesome to begin with but I had all kinds of playmates. We were all in the same boat. We all had a good relationship, playing, we were all somewhat from the same mold. I as a person appreciated that sanctuary. I had three meals a day, good wholesome food... I lived in a dormitory. All the laundry was done at the school, the girls did all that. Domestic training, actually it was an industrial school... I was the one selected to do the barbering. I had a professional come in and I think teach three or four of us to cut hair. We had the hydraulic chairs. They provided a good training area for barbering. Of course, when I went to the army, I cut hair. I accumulated quite a bit of money. Every time someone wanted money, they'd come to me and borrow it. I always had money... It was all regimented. We all marched. When we gathered to march, we were all inspected by one of the older students that came from the big boys down. They had this kind of position to keep track of us. When we lined up, you had to have clean hands. They would check your hair, your hair had to be combed. They were disciplined... Of course, if your hands were dirty, they would rap them with a light stick."*

"Then after breakfast we would get back to our dormitory... and get ready for school...And they would march us over, we were in formation. There was a cleanliness inspection again...we would do almost a full eight hours of school." They were inspected for cleanliness before meals all day long. Meals were served in a big bowl, and everyone would help themselves. There were six to eight children sitting at the table. "The girls would be on that side and we would be on this side. And they had girls up in the middle that would serve us. This again was their domestic training... The older boys would work on the farm, and they would work in the boiler house... They had a carpenter shop. They were supposed to go in and learn how to use tools... They would do repair work on the school, paint windows and repair chairs... Then they had agriculture training, tending crops and that sort of thing. They had a big dairy farm, so they worked in the dairy barns. The clothes were all brought in, they were government made. I know they were all the same. They would put your number on the back. So, when they did the laundry... the matron for the small boys and small girls, she had to match all the laundry. She would get the laundry and fold it and put it in the cubicle there..." Jeff was a bed wetter but the only repercussion was that they slept in a wet bed. The sheets were changed the next day.

Jeff reported he was involved in activities that were not part of the scheduled school program. Jeff and a few of his friends would sneak out at night and go fishing and one night he stole a flashlight among other things with his friends from a local store. "They had these officers, the older students, they would come around and check, do a bed check. Everyone would have to be in bed. Course after they're gone, we'd sneak out. We'd do things, we would go down to the river and fish and stay out all night... We'd sneak into town. They knew we were government kids. Another bad habit I had, I stole. I would go to the hardware store. I couldn't keep my hands off the knives and flashlights... The disciplinarian was out there walking, looking for people who stole some flashlights. He knew what room it came from and he would come upstairs and take our flashlights. Next day, they would give us a hard whipping... I saw nothing wrong with that. I knew I would get a licking if I did something wrong and that was wrong... We would go to the mill and skate on that ice... In the Spring, we would go into the river and get on this ice and float down the river."

Jeff was asked to explain his worse and best memories at the school. *"Most of them were good. To me that was a godsend. I don't know what I would have done if it wasn't for that Indian school... I really can't think of anything bad. Everything they insisted on me doing, I should do. I should wake up at a certain time in the morning, clean up and have breakfast, go to school. You would expect that. If you don't do it now, the truant officer is after you. And cleanliness was practiced. Good housing and dry clean linen... We played a lot of football. The big boys would get a team together. We'd play against each other. We used to make our own football... I think they should have had the gym open all the time. We all had to participate in athletics, gymnastics... we had a qualified physical trainer. I think we went to the gym three times a week... We had good equipment... Why anyone would knock it, maybe they had it better at home but not with me. Actually, there was five of us in Muskegon area where other families didn't have suitable homes. They had to go to the children's home too after the Indian School. So, I was there until about eighth grade at the children's home and then part of ninth grade..."*

My moving from the Indian school to the public school, I didn't have any problems... I was physically able, if you want to antagonize me you would be in trouble... The Probate Court, they wasn't interested in me, somebody wanted their oats sewed in the Spring. The Probate Court released me to work for my room and board at this farm East of Muskegon. When I look back on it that was terrible doing something like that to a minor. Didn't even let me finish the ninth grade.*" He worked there for two years.

He lived on his own, and then he worked for another family. The male head of household at this farm was previously employed as a superintendent of a school. *"They were educated people. They weren't teaching then. They were strictly farmers..."* He went hunting with the owner of the farm. They treated him with respect and provided him with his needs such as clothing. They also encouraged him to go back to school, and he did. Jeff successfully graduated as the valedictorian of his class from high school. *"I was a good basketball player in my high school. I had to work, too... I had a good relationship with my fellow students, in fact because I was a couple of years older... I was a good student without trying... My sisters, they all came to my graduation."* He was asked about his relationship to other extended family members such as aunts and uncles. *"I visited them from time to time. We had a cordial relationship. They treat me all right."*

After serving time in the service, Jeff attended Michigan State University on the GI Bill. He attended for three years but he said he lacked the ambition to make a determination about his future. He looked upon this time period as taking the easy way out. Jeff married his wife in 1939 and has remained married ever since. Jeff obtained a position at General Motors until his retirement a few years ago. He referred to General Motors as "Generous Motors." They paid him well and he was able to advance up the ladder. He said his wife's main duty was to raise the children and she did so until the children graduated from high school. They have seven children, whom he talked about to a large degree. Jeff was focused for a while on his children's college and their success with employment and the acquisition of material things such as their nice homes. His son has given him many nice things such as the gas grill that was on his porch. Jeff showed me his hunting blind his daughter built for him.

Jeff has participated in a variety of sports throughout his lifetime. Many of his children were involved in sports, too. He was currently a member of a bowling team. He stressed he didn't drink alcohol. Jeff has gone to Pow wows and his wife has collected Native American art items such as baskets. He also said Native Americans must marry other Native Americans. We ended the interview by eating apples in his living room while he discussed turkey hunting.

Interview # 2: Doris from Sault Ste. Marie, Michigan

Doris was born in Sault Ste. Marie, Michigan ninety-one years ago. She was sent to the boarding school in Mt. Pleasant when she was six and stayed until she reached high school age. Her father died serving in the army at Fort Brady when she was two. Her grandparents lived in Sault Ste. Marie a couple of blocks from her family home. Her mother was raising her on her own when she was placed at the boarding school. She said she liked the church services. Her mother would go to the boarding school with things she bought for her. Doris had a special place while at the school to store these gifts, but Her mother died in a car accident when Doris was nine. Following her attendance of the school, she went to the Catholic school in Sault Ste. Marie. She liked learning more about the Catholic religion.

Doris started the interview by stating she was picky about how she liked her house maintained. This was explained in great detail. *"Nobody satisfies me. I am very different. I am very fussy."* She fell on her arm a couple of weeks before this interview was conducted. She was receiving physical therapy and there were people who came to the home to clean and provide assistance in other ways.

Doris explained some of her experiences at the Mt. Pleasant boarding school. *"When I was in Mt. Pleasant I didn't have to do any detail work... They had me just do the employees' table... Detail was like when you were out washing the dishes at the machine and hauling garbage and stuff like that. They had a special place for the employees' table... We had to get up and get ready to go to the dining room for our breakfast. I used to like to do fun stuff like dancing... Sometimes they would have a drum to go along with the other music... I was a good little dancer. I loved getting on the stage and singing. They would have celebrations like for your birthday. It was the same way, where you did the laundry for the school. I did the employees' laundry... I would do the dishes after and I had everything cleaned up... oh they had everything, meat and good vegetables. Of course, it was different at the employees' table... the salads were made individually which I got to do a lot of that... So, I always liked that..."*

She was asked about friendships at the boarding school. She mentioned the children who received money from their tribe. They received approximately three to four hundred dollars and she described some of the things they bought with it. She did not explain any activities she participated in with these children. Doris went on to discuss some of her favorite experiences at the boarding school: *"I liked to work in the dispensary. That's where I got a lot of experience... We made our own clothes, too. Like I said, I made my own uniform for graduation... There was a couple that came from the Sault here. And their crying wouldn't stop. 'Oh I miss my daddy.' Couldn't do anything with her. She was just a big baby and turned out that way."* There was discussion about the teaching staff and the quality of education provided at the school. *"The teachers, they were good. They would come from different states... Some of the children would have to stay over to brush up a little more on their school work, very, very efficient."*

Doris liked to do things when she was at home with her mother such as sledding in the wintertime and roller skating. She loves music.

Doris and her husband had five children. Her husband was deceased. She discussed in depth about her children's jobs and their possessions such as nice homes and beautiful cars. Things were pointed out in the home her adult children have purchased for her and she would discuss the price of some of the items. Her husband liked to fish but she doesn't trust eating the fish now. She and her husband played catch in their yard. He was a good baseball player. She didn't have time to do many fun things with him, but when her children were younger, they went camping on occasion. She was asked how she learned how to do things and she said she just knew. *"I don't know. Aunt Nettie didn't teach me. No, it just came to me, everything did...it was just my way of doing things."* Doris lived with her Aunt Nettie when she went to the Catholic school in Sault Ste. Marie.

She described further who she was as a person. *"It was in me to work. I was like a slave. I didn't mind it at all. I didn't feel like I was a slave. If I wasn't doing something, I wasn't happy. I just wanted to do something all the time. I used to go over to grandma's, my husband's grandma. And we used to go and help her, and she had a stairway with no carpeting, no nothing, just wood floor stuff... I used scrub those white for her. She would be so happy when I came over and help her iron. Because she took in washings you know... She would give us a jar of homemade jam and half a dozen eggs. And that's the way she would pay me instead of money."*

Doris focused a lot on household chores and related much of her life to the satisfaction she received by accomplishing tasks in a manner she deemed acceptable. She led the conversation to a discussion about her late husband. She described visits she had received from her late husband. At the end of the interview, Doris was given some photographs taken of the Mt. Pleasant boarding school. She stared at the photographs. She appeared to be happy to get these photos. The interview ended with Doris describing the loss of many memorabilia during a recent house fire.

Interview # 3: Fred from Sault Ste. Marie, Michigan.

Fred was born and raised in Sault Ste. Marie, Michigan and he was in his early eighties during the time this interview was conducted.

He came from a large family, which lived in poverty when he was a child. He attended the Mt. Pleasant boarding school in 1927 or 1928 for one year. He made reference to how tough those times were. It was the year before the "Depression" hit the country. Fred spent a lot of time with his extended family such as his aunts and grandmothers. He explained the making of maple syrup and how the elders, such as his grandpa, had made it in the past. He commented what a wonderful cook his aunt was and said his grandmother had a sanitation business with which he assisted. His father left to move to the Detroit area when Fred was in his teens, and his mother and grandmother raised him after that. Every summer, his family and extended family members set up camp in the Strongs area and pick blueberries all summer. That was one of their main sources of income for the family. Fred would listen to music that was played by local musicians while at the camp. "*All Indians had a little talent, to play some guitar or this or that.*" He explained parts of the history of the area.

Fred described with some detail his experiences at the Mt. Pleasant boarding school. "*I was only six years old when I went there. I stayed in the little boys' dormitory. One side was for people who didn't wet the bed. Course we were up in age and we didn't wet the bed. There were smaller ones on the other side. There was a bunch of cows. There was the M.I.L.K. company and they had a place where they raised their own beef. They had older boys tending the cows... Every morning you would line up just like the army at attention. You would learn how to drill. Rear march, squad right, same thing as in the army... There was a military training. It was built like a military fort, like Fort Brady... The bake shop, it was a great big place with board tables. Again, it was just like I was in the army... They would call your name too and you if you weren't there they would call you AWOL... The potatoes, they had rows and rows of potatoes. We would be picking up the potatoes and throwing them on the wagons... I can't remember ever getting any sugar... I had a runny ear. I would go to the dispensary. It was like a hospital... I had to go there every day and they had to drain that out for me.*"

Fred was asked what his favorite experiences were at the boarding school. He said "*Steal apples. After you got out of school... you had your chores for that day... You would eat because you were always hungry... Like I said about the bake shop, hollow out that bread and put some lard and some sugar in it. They tasted like coconut cream pie back in them days. You never had sweets... Never see no milk or sugar."*

He would catch the train and go exploring when he was a child living in Sault Ste. Marie. Movies were only ten cents and bread was two cents a loaf. Public school was not a pleasant experience for him. *"I went and I quit... When you were Indian back in them days you just kept your place... I always went to school four or five of us at a time... It was a group anyway. We never in no trouble either... A pair of pants were only $1.25 back then... But in those days, the kids they had these ties, these shoes, they looked pretty good in them days... Anyways I was designated to be the lead singer...How are you going to school if you ain't got nothing to wear... I never showed. She was disappointed... (His grade school teacher). I was ashamed."* His worst memory from his childhood was trying to get clothes to wear to school. He was threatened with reform school, so he decided to try and go to school as much as possible. One of his public school teachers sold him the home that he still lives in for what he was being charged for one month's rent.

We discussed if anyone spoke the Ojibwe language. *"My grandma, that's where I missed the boat... They all talked Indian. We went away on that because we didn't want that at that time, you know. They were called savage when they were going to school... The Indians back in them days, all they wanted to do was put them in the bush to cut pulp wood... The job would charge thirty-five to forty cents... Salt pork would maybe cost fifty cents... They got done in the Spring of the year, they got nothing, they owed the job..."* He explained further about some of his extended family members who spoke the language and participated in traditional practices. *"Grandma, right on Cedar Street, it was quite a little street for Indians. They would all come down... they would all sit down by the two big elm trees... They'd make a smudge and get it going... they would all talk Indian. We would all run away. We could have learned it easy. Nobody in the area wanted to..."*

When Fred served in the army, he was recognized for how highly trained he was. *"I was called in 1943... Lieutenant Peterson was a real American Company C. Reviewing the three squads of us anyway. I was at attention, and he stood right in front of me and he said 'private' and I said yes sir. 'I see you got your training down in Mt.*

Pleasant.' Yes sir. 'Did you ever go to West Point?' Then he gave me an at ease. No, sir. 'Where did you get your training at?' I said that I went to a government Indian school in Mt. Pleasant, Michigan. You know I think I could have been sergeant right then and there, but I was afraid of them guys... I knew all the commands you know. That was a good experience you know down in Mt. Pleasant."

Adam, the medicine man who came to the Sault Ste. Marie Tribe of Chippewa Indians, requested Fred to play the drum while Adam was providing care to tribal clients. *"Its like a prayer... You know how to bang bang bang by listening to him. He said I was ok on that drum. I got a little Indian in me, so I guess I know how to pound on that. I did that quite a few times for him... he wanted me to go every day..."* This commitment had to be given up because he had to stay home with his wife to provide care for her.

Fred married his wife in 1943. She was of European American descent. They had fifteen children. He described in detail how well each one of his adult children were doing. He explained their material items such as their nice homes and the vehicles they owned. Many of his children provide assistance to them in many ways such as preparing meals for them and buying him a truck. Fred's wife was ill when the interview was conducted, and he explained what was happening to her in regards to her healing process. His wife was introduced during the interview.

Fred showed me different types of fishing equipment utilized by Native American fishermen. He looked at pictures of the Mt. Pleasant boarding school and he pointed out the purpose of the buildings. Taking a walk around Fred's yard ended the interview and various points of interest were discussed.

Holy Childhood Boarding School

Interview #4: Kent from Sugar Island

Kent was in his mid-fifties during the time of the interview, and he began by relaying information about the history of his family of origin. His father, grandfather and uncles were fishermen and his family lived on a reservation in Ontario, Canada. Later on, they were allotted a plot of land approximately 160 to 250 acres in Gros Cap, which is directly across from Bay Mills. The land was considered useless. The government placed more and more restrictions on fishing and the lumbering businesses. His father was unable to provide for his family and that was the main reason why Kent was sent to the Holy Childhood boarding school in Harbor Springs.

He believed one of the reasons why the family suffered from poverty was linked to their Ojibwe heritage. According to Kent, his family of origin could not be honest about their heritage. *"Because what happened when I was little. We moved here and because of the situation then, it wasn't good to be an Anisaahnabe. So, my aunts were anything but Anishaanabe. They were French. They were Italian. They were anything anybody that kind of had a dark color to their skin. That's what they had. They wouldn't hire my uncles at Algoma Steel or any place like that because they were Anishaanabe...It's like the language. They couldn't speak their own language. They could speak French. The French were accepted but people still looked down their noses at the French a little bit. English was the A number one thing."*

Kent attended the boarding school for approximately seven and one-half years along with four of his siblings. He was approximately six years of age when he started. He described many experiences there throughout the interview. *"We were called boarders. The people that were not were called day scholars. The day scholars had a different regimen\ of doing things than we did. We would start about 5:00 in the morning. All the kids would get ready to go and be with the nuns... So, we would all go to church with the nuns. Then after the chapel we would come back and make our beds and do our chores and then we would go to breakfast...before we went to class, we had to go to church again...It was a line to go play. It was a line to go to bed, a line to brush your teeth... We would all stand in line down these halls. The girls on one end and the boys on another. We would stand facing one another, no talking... After lunch we would go out. They had a playground for the girls and a playground for the boys... We would get in line to go have our supper and we would get to, even when we were eating it was to be quiet After the meal was done the girls would go and do their thing. The boys had to wash all the dishes... The girls cooked and the boys washed the dishes."*

Kent explained some of things they did to entertain themselves at the school. They put on little skits and sang and played instruments such as the harmonica. Those friendships were important to Kent. He recalled three boys who remained his friends throughout his entire boarding school experience. There were various restrictions implied through obscure ways. *"We were not allowed to use our own tongue. Nobody ever came to us and said you can't speak that. It was an unspoken rule...The nuns were really disciplinarians. Some of them were pretty mean...There's actually two nuns that stand out in my mind from all the years that I have been there. One of the nun's name was Sister.... She was the meanest individual I ever ran into in my entire whole life. She was sadistic. The other nun was in charge of the senior boys. Her name was Sister...."*

Kent explained how every Friday or Saturday night they would show a movie in the girls' playroom. They all had to line up to get a chair, which were stored in the basement. The first one usually got the best chair. He said this was important because the simple things like getting the best chair or having a good pair of pants to wear was where his pleasure was derived from. He described an incident when he was the first one to go get his chair and he was forced physically to give up his chair to one of the nun's favorite boarders. Kent wrapped himself around the chair and the banister to the stairway and the nun managed to pry the chair away and sent him flying down the stairs. She turned out the lights and had him sit in the dark at the bottom of the stairs in the basement. She closed the door behind him. He described the basement as having "itty bitty" lights and it seemed like a mile long. It was like looking down a dark tunnel. Without the lights, it was even scarier. *"I think I was probably seven. It scared the hell out of me. I didn't care. I stayed right there until she finally came and said I could go. So, I didn't get to see the movie or anything like that. I thought about that, the things that affect your life. You know the way you do certain things. I always had this, even now, it grips me if I have to go outside in the pitch black... I think when things happen like that to you and your attitude. If you were a little boy, you grew up damn fast. And you know that there is no mommy and there is no daddy. There's nobody, just you... so you better stand up and learn how to fight and take care of yourself... Then I became one mean son-of-a-bitch."*

He was asked what his best experience was and he said, *"My best experience, going home. My greatest experiences... was when my parents would come to see us. My parents would only come to see us at Easter and at Christmas. Sometimes that was it. I could hardly wait to go home...my most favorite memory of my childhood was my grandmother. She was a little brown lady... I remember the time when she came to see me at the boarding school. My grandma came there once or twice but I will never forget it."*

Kent explained that living in another world such as the boarding school was foreign to him. At the same time, when he went home during the summer months, he would spend most of the time with his grandparents. *"When I was in the boarding school I was trained to live in another world other than an Anishaanabe world. I didn't know what my world was when I was here. Because in my mind this was my home because it was where you come and visit for the summer and you go away. Is that your home? I would come here and maybe be with my parents maybe for about two to three weeks then I would go to Gros Cap Ontario with my grandmother and grandfather. And that's where I learned about my heritage more. My grandma was a full blooded Anishaanabe. And when I learned the language the only words I knew were from my grandma and my grandpa."*

Kent participated in traditional activities with his grandparents and other extended family members and continued to do so with his Native American family and friends. During the interview, he spoke the various Ojibwe words and phrases he had learned. His goal was to learn one phrase or word on a daily basis. He explained how the Anishaanabeg (plural) traditionally cooked their meals and tied his explanation with a legend. Story telling was a tool used to educate Anishaanabe children by parents, grandparents and other extended family members. Kent said he had stories he wanted to share with me during another visit.

The interview was ended by further explanation about the things in which he was involved in such as sweatlodge ceremonies, which included a water drum. *"The water drum supposedly could cure you for a couple of miles. Just that little tiny drum."* Kent continued to immerse himself in the Ojibwe culture by participating and associating with his Anishaanabe family. *"It was like somebody gave me a culture. Just a made up culture of somebody else's. It was like a delusion of another race... So, I am still going through that to change back. I am being filtered. So, that's how I learned was by doing it."*

Interview #5: Yulanda from Petoskey

Yulanda was raised primarily by her father and her uncle in the Petoskey area and was in her late forties during the time of interview. Her mother left and did not return except only to visit on occasion. Her uncle shared a piece of property with her father. Babysitters were hired to watch over her and her siblings while her father was at work. However, the babysitters ended up drinking alcohol and abandoning them. One of her siblings went to a neighbor's home because they were cold and hungry. The uncle was not home at the time. The neighbor contacted the authorities. Individuals came into the home and cleaned and bathed the children, and provided necessary supplies such as food and started a fire in the wood stove. The court ordered her and her siblings to be placed in the Holy Childhood Boarding School in Harbor Springs. Her father was ordered to pay child support in the form of money or food supplies to the boarding school staff. Yulanda attended for seven years and each year she went home and stayed with her father during the summer months.

Her father had a lot of support from family members. "*My uncle would see to it that we ate and we were very, very lucky to have him... He had cousins who helped him. We learned how to dye eggs, did Christmas things. When we finally got to go home, you know, he had cousins who helped us with what we should be doing. The only time he stumbled when it came to personal needs with us girls... I used to go with him on some of the night jobs. I was fishing when he was working on some of the houses and doing extra jobs... He taught all the things that guys should know but we were girls...He was a plumber.*"

Chores were shared at home. She was in charge of home repairs and her siblings were in charge of other household tasks. "*Holy Childhood taught us the cooking part, house cleaning and all the other things... Someone donated bolts and bolts of cloth one year. We all had skirts and uniforms that were all the same. Sometimes we would embroider pillowcases and things like that. In the summertime we were not supervised. My dad would say stay in the yard and we knew the perimeters and we would stay within those perimeters and do what he said... We played together and we stayed in the yard together. We did everything together.*"

Her father used art and stories to teach her and her siblings. These activities continued to be carried out today with her children. Yulanda told two legends about how the porcupine got their quills during the interview. (Refer to Appendix 1). They used to go around and visit their Anishaanabe friends and family. She referred to this as making the rounds. This was still being practiced today with her children. Humor was an important component during her childhood. She recalled many times her family used humor as a way of providing entertainment for one another.

She was asked about the Ojibwe language. Yulanda reported that she didn't find out until she was sixteen that her dad spoke the language. Her uncle Pete came to the door and asked to speak with her dad and they spoke to one another in Ojibwe. "*I sensed right away that there was something up. They had this conversation... Then it occurred to me that they were speaking their own language. There was a girl that went to school there and knew not a word of English. They beat her if she would talk in her language. She would hang her head. My dad said the same thing. He would not teach us. When I heard an elder speaking the language, it took me right back to when I was a kid. I was impressed.*"

Her father was generous when it came to their friends. "*He didn't care if there were thirteen kids in the house. He would feed them.*" Her father drank alcohol with his friends and family. She started her marriage and raising her kids by drinking alcohol every weekend with her husband. Then she changed her focus to raising her kids, and on the weekends would take up to twenty-three children to the movie theater and they would participate in other fun activities. Both her father and the staff at the Holy Childhood boarding school promoted reading. She reads everything she can get her hands on, she reported during the interview.

The educational portion of the boarding school experience was not always positive for Yulanda. "*I had a hard time with math, adding and subtracting. It was because I think that I was traumatized back then. Now when it comes to numbers and math, I don't want to do it till this day... I have turned down job promotions 'cause I don't want to work with budgets. They scare me away. I am willing to work overtime and whatever else to do my job, but I don't want to work with budgets... I have more hair on the left side of my head than I do the right because they would drag me around by the hair. The hair was pulled out of my head. Plus, they would grab you by the hair and slam you into the chalkboard. I was up close to the chalkboard a lot of the times."*

Yulanda reported alliances that were built while attending the boarding school and later on in her adult life. *"We would cross sympathize. We would know it and we could feel it and we could sense it. When they were yelling at you, trying to make you think and do that number on the board... you could hear and see and the classroom behind you. They sided with you. It was very simple things. You might hear a sssss sound. Maybe one person might do it, but you could hear it. You could hear a little murmur or you could hear a tap tap tap sound... Like there was a bed wetter and we would sympathize. They would be drug by their hair or forced to stand out on the fire escape odraggedutside and wrap their wet soaked sheets around them, you know even if it was wintertime... We would say quick make your bed and throw the towels on them to soak up the urine. We had a sign language where we could look at each other and agree and disagree... We were held together by being in the same boat..."*

Yulanda demonstrated a form of resistance by not crying in front of the nuns. *"She grabbed a board and beat me with that board... Why don't you hit me back. I was always respectful to older people... She really wanted me to cry. I would not cry. It was not until I was in bed alone that I cried. I was sent to bed without any supper... A girl was sneaking me raw carrots. She was working in the kitchen... Well, she went upstairs and got a beating on the stairs... I usually got a poking in the chest. They knew when I was at an early age that I would not back down. I would not look at them directly... I would not bend or break or be submissive."*

The older girls were placed in charge of taking care of the younger girls. This was part of their training as a preparation for returning home. They could in part assist with taking care of their younger siblings. *"When I went there from grades first to fourth, you were basically a junior. You pretty much played along with kids and learn how to play and learn how to socialize. Then when you were in the fourth grade, they started teaching you buttons. How to sew them on. In the fifth grade you were given a girl to take care of. In fifth grade you became a senior and the girl you take care of is a junior... It would make their work a little easier and we would sew their clothes. Made sure their hair was clean and combed..."*

Yulanda explained other boarding school experiences. *"There was fifty of us packed into two classrooms. There were two grades in each room. One teacher would teach first and second grade. She would start out with one grade in the morning and then the other half would have to do homework or read. Then she would go to the other grade and work with them. She was working back and forth in that classroom from 9:00 until 3:00. If there was a disruption with one kid, she would spend ten to fifteen minutes yelling at him and knocking him around. There was a lot of that, that got knocked around a lot... If there was colds or viruses or things going around, you would jump in line and get a clean handkerchief. During that time, too, you had to jump in line if you had to take medicine. Like everybody got cod-liver oil from the same tablespoon. All fifty of us would have our mouths opened wide."*

She was asked what happened to runaways. *"They would be beaten by the nuns, and they would be turned over to the brothers and they would beat them. Then they were turned over to the security and she beat them, and the students were allowed to beat them too."* Meals were eaten in silence and activities were censored. *"You were required to write a letter home at least every other week. Your letters were censored. You would turn it in and she would read it. If she didn't like it, she would scratch it up. You would have to take it back and you would have to rewrite it. I couldn't tell them that they were being mean to me or hitting me or anything like that. Things we would write about would be, we went for walks and we would have meat for supper. Sometimes like deer meat you know. Really bland letters. So, you wouldn't get them in trouble... Books that were brought in were censored. Movies were censored."*

Religion was a big part of what was practiced at the Holy Childhood boarding school. *"They pushed religion. I accepted what they were telling me, and I believed it and I really did pray hard... The only time that I had trouble was my first confession... We used to make up things for confession. Because we were actually basically really good kids. The religion part wasn't too bad until I got older. When I was in eighth grade and we were getting ready to leave the school, sister... told us about kids being raped and murdered. So, when I was in eighth grade, she was the first one to give us a reality check. The boys are going to want sex and you girls have to say no. Another nun told us that she was a nun for penance for killing her sister."* This was an accident when she was cutting wood with her sister. *"There was an Indian one there at one time. I found out later that she was a cousin. She looked after me."*

The boarding school experience impacted Yulanda in a multitude of ways. *"The Holy Childhood experience set us in a schedule. To this day, on Saturday, we still clean. We learned some things at Holy Childhood that were rigid that I haven't broken. I stayed with that. When I got to high school, I was so rigid that they thought that I was stuck up and stupid because I didn't respond to them. I never learned how to socialize with friends... They would talk about movies, music, just normal teenage stuff. It didn't compute with me. I didn't fit in. I think every kid that came from the Holy Childhood was like that. We went out into the world, and it was chaos. They took away our ability to make decisions. They made them for us. If some kids said party, they would party. They just went with the flow. So many kids got pregnant and drunk because they went with the crowd and became alcoholics you know because of the school experience... I just sat there until they called ya. If they didn't call on you for six months, I was fine with that. You would get graded on participation... I never skipped school. I never had the nerve to skip school. When I was sick, the nurse would say you are very sick and I would be at school and they would say we are going to take you home and they would give me a ride."*

Yulanda addressed the high dropout rate of Indian kids, as she referred to them. *"When I started ninth grade, I think there was about fifteen Indian kids in the school in Charlevoix. Just about all of them dropped out except for three... So, the dropout rate was high."*

Her two sons attended the Holy Childhood boarding school. One of her sons resented the experience. She explained the history behind the school and its closure in 1983. *"...I worked to keep it opened and turn it into an alternative school. Tribes let them build that church and let their children go there as long as they would educate their children. If you are going to shut the school down, give the school back to the people."* There was a scandal involving a few boys who were vandals. According to her, they were out of control. *"The nuns got fed up and laid hands on them and the kids reported them... It was a generation after generation going to that school. I was a part of that history part."* She was asked how many generations went to the boarding school and she reported three generations, her parents, herself and her sons. *"Yeah, on my mother's side and my father's side... I was a survivor..."*

We ended the interview by discussing the bond many have who attended the school. Many people, she reported, share the same bond who attended the Holy Childhood boarding school. *"You went to Holy Childhood and so did I. It didn't matter what age. A sixty year old would come up to me and say I went to Holy Childhood and I would say did you know that bonds us right away."*

Interview #6 Brenda from St. Ignace

Brenda was raised in St. Ignace by both parents and was in her early seventies during the time the interview was conducted. Poverty was not an issue for her family because, according to her, both of her parents worked. She worked while she was in high school for extended family members at the Moose Lodge as a waitress. Her father was away a lot working on boats. Brenda inherited her Ojibwe ethnicity from her father's side while her mother was of Polish descent. This created some issues regarding discrimination. Her father attended the Holy Childhood boarding school and to maintain this tradition, his children were sent there for approximately one year. Two of his children were not accepted the following year due to the light coloring of their skin and hair. Brenda and one of her brothers had darker skin and darker hair. Her sister had a lighter complexion.

Brenda described the visits to her maternal grandmother's home. *"We had to visit her mother every summer... The only time we were allowed to go inside was to get to bed or to eat. We also had to sit at the end of the table. We had to use tin plates and the crummiest looking forks you ever saw. She did not want savages in her house... She would have our uncles down there every night but she wouldn't let us in the house. Now my sister could go in the house."*

Positive involvement existed with her paternal relatives. *"Dad's mother was there. Uncle Charlie and his brother and sister, Aunt Lillie, and my grandma and my brothers and sisters. My grandma gave me a book of poems. It had all kinds of poems..."* Her father's relatives were the ones who were mostly involved in her upbringing. She sadly reported that her brother died in a car accident some time ago.

One of the family traditions involved the children walking to church during lent, rain or shine. It was approximately seven to ten miles. They had a car and the neighbors would offer to take them to church. Her mother insisted they walk. Brenda did not know her mother played the piano until she was in her twenties. She recalled her father embroidering and sewing. He had a sense of humor and would tease her mother. Some of her fondest memories as a child involved playing outside with her siblings and friends. They used big pans to slide down hills in the wintertime and they climbed trees.

Brenda explained some of her boarding school experiences. *"We really starved. Breakfast, I don't know what it was they gave us, but there was no sugar or cream on it or anything. Bugs were in it, and they would make us eat that...I don't remember ever having a decent meal down there. The only thing that I do remember is that sometimes on Sunday they would give us a treat. They would give us a slice of bread with syrup and an apple...Mom and dad use to bring in tomatoes and they used to bring in apples. Kids never got any of that stuff..."* *"I don't know how many times they put kerosene on our hair. It was to kill lice. Then we would keep it on all day... Everybody smelled like kerosene... They weren't nice down there. I know that one time one of my brothers threw a ball and a car went by and it broke the window...She made us lie... We used to have a big Christmas... All the visiting priests and nuns would come in. They were usually too drunk to come to the Christmas parade. And they had rooms for them. Now they wouldn't sleep in separate rooms either. They had this one room upstairs... Some of us would have to give, well after these parties, used to have to give these rooms a good cleaning. It smelled like alcohol. We had to wash all those glasses and all those plates. You should see the pictures that were on the wall, on the blackboard. Now, these were not pictures that you would want little kids to see..."*

Brenda said she did not like the nuns and resented that they put on airs like they were good and proper. *"I would see those nuns and priests going up there so darn holy. Acting like holy terrors. We were young but we still knew what was going on. But we couldn't say nothing. They would tell us not to. You don't say anything... My mother wouldn't believe me anyways... Dad would have believed us but mom never would have."*

Brenda was twelve years of age when she attended the school. *"I knew how to cook before I got there. I was baking bread when I was nine years old.... Didn't do any sewing down there... We did a lot of singing because we had to sing in the choir, in Latin..."*

She and her allies planned and carried acts of resistance during her stay at the boarding school. *"You know what we used to do, we use to take and grab a piece of paper usually toilet paper and we would sing in the choir, and we would shoot it at the wings in their hats. We would throw things that the hats would hold. Sometimes we would throw gum. They made us wear these stupid silk hats... With those white blouses and black skirts and those white silk hats and we had to wear hose. We used to cut and rip those hose and wear those to church on Sunday. Nuns didn't catch us, you see, have to go to communion every Sunday. We would have those cute little silk hats and we would put them on and go to communion and throw our heads back like that and the hats would fall down. They would get so mad at us. We did that a lot."*

"This nun had false teeth and she would be up there singing and her teeth would fall out... She would make us slap our own faces. Now that was funny. She would say slap your face and slap it hard.."

The topic changed to what happened to the children who ran away from the school. *"I don't know but they would always bring them back... They had to clean the black marks off the floors...You could eat off the floors..."*

She was asked about the teaching practices at the school. *"School was good. I liked my teacher, too. Some of the kids didn't like her. She was stern."* Some of the fun things they did at school was going tobogganing and going for walks. One of the worst memories of the school besides the food was cleaning the windows. They had to clean the third story windows. *"I was so scared that I was going to fall."*

The interview ended with a discussion about her grandson who was living at her home. He seemed to be the focal point of her life. She was making fry bread and said that her mother used to burn the fry bread when she made it.

Interview #7: Tim from Sault Ste. Marie, Michigan

Tim lived with his family in Canada during his childhood and was in his late forties during the time the of interview. His father was a member of the Ojibwe tribe (known as the First Nation) from Garden River, Ontario. They moved to Gros Cap, Ontario later in his childhood. The government placed more restrictions on their fishing rights, which infringed on feeding their family. They resided on the reservation and his father went to the residential school in Canada. *"The tribes were beginning to make land settlements, restructure and reorganize... So, my dad took on the tradition of being independent for as long as he could... Then he went to work at the steel plant. I think he quit fishing the same time we were at the boarding school."* Tim's mother was an Ojibwe from Sugar Island. His family faced many difficulties such as alcoholism, suicide, domestic violence and poverty, and his father drank a lot. One child after another were being born to what became a large family.

His parents liked to play music, dance, and had other talents such as gymnastics. His father served in WWII and was an honored soldier. He had difficulty supporting his children so some of them were sent to the Holy Childhood boarding school. *"The boarding school would have a place for us, and food. Then they could afford to take care of the babies."* Tim attended for one year and was told beforehand that he would be able to be with his siblings at the school. He was not permitted to see them, which had a long-lasting negative effect on him.

Tim shared additional details about his childhood. *"Lots of storytelling around the fire... Some of the stories, the ones we remember the most, were the scary ones like the ones about bear walking... Another story was about spirits of the water. Not to go in a direction if a hand comes out of the water. .. They would all tell stories about growing up and what they did together as kids... The oral tradition was our tradition. We did a lot of talking about things...We went hunting, fishing, swimming a lot. We were in the woods all the time. We cut wood every day. Hauled water every day. Fished just about every day. Uncles would bring deer, moose, and bear meat. When we were old enough, we would go and get meat. There was squirrel and rabbit."*

The boarding school experience was explained in detail. Tim only attended for one year, but that made a negative impact on his life. *"The boarding school experience damaged me greatly. I got really sick there. After five years after I left there, I had to get penicillin shots for what they called Rheumatic fever... They exposed us to all the other kids that came in that may have had things... I was five when I left home. I turned six in October... I was still pretty young to go... I got very ill. I guess you could call it homesick. It was a combination of being homesick. I wanted to be with my brothers and* sisters, and I wasn't... I think I developed more sickness because I was emotionally distraught... It was a suffering place... Then for eight years after that, I was in and out of the hospital trying to recover basically. My heart was very sick for almost ten years. You were there to be disciplined and educated. They did that to us. They certainly educated us and disciplined us... A lot of kids died there. A lot of kids thrived there. But for a kid like me, it nearly killed me. Home wasn't the greatest compared to other places, but there were things that we managed to value and enjoy while we were there."

Tim talked more about his boarding school experience. "It was structured religious ceremony ritual. Then you would learn how to be a soldier of God. Catholicism was heavy. You had to learn the Stations of the Cross, purgatory, communion." He was asked how he was being raised at home concerning spiritual practices. "We were being raised traditional. We were being raised outside. We were hunting, fishing, learning the wilds of Canada... We didn't kill animals just to kill them, we ate them."

He described some of his worst experiences while at the boarding school. "The worst experience was being disciplined. Being made to wear a pissy sheet because I peed the bed. I had to wear a sheet and a diaper in the food line to go and eat. The worst thing was having great big sores all over my head and my body after being inoculated... That, combined with some of the missionary films they were showing us about going over to these leper colonies being a missionary. You were going there to die to save these people. I thought I had leprosy. The impact it had on me was that it made me introverted, a lack of confidence. I wasn't encouraged to grow. I was deteriorating... They didn't feed us well or clothe us well. I remember going into this one area where they had blankets, shoes, clothes. We had to go in and find our stuff to wear. A lot of stuff was given by other orphanages or hospitals. From what I understand, it wasn't clean."

"I would have much rather been at home where mom and dad were fighting, drinking and there was domestic violence, abuse between them than to go through being institutionalized in a place where they tell you that you're evil. You're totally evil and nothing is ever going to save you. So, you may as well give yourself over to God and die however that God deems, because if you don't the devils got you, fear of the devil. What they made me afraid of was the dark."

"There were some parlor times, where you would go and did

things, social functions. Watching plays, I guess, they got ready for plays, musicals. I don't remember much about the rest of it... I remember one night a kid hemorrhaged to death in the bathroom. I walked in and saw it."

When he was asked if there were any positive experiences, he said there were only negative ones. The positives in his childhood ended up being the negatives. When he was participating in fun things with his friends, he recalled that if he hurt himself in any way he ended up in the hospital.

Stories around the campfire were addressed in more detail to explain the difference between these teachings and the teachings at the boarding school. *"You combine that with the Ojibwe stories, the stuff we had heard, we had heard them around the fire. We saw laughing going along with it. They would tickle us, and they would wrestle us and somebody would throw us in the water. That was playful. This other teaching was you are no good. There's nothing good about you."*

Tim was asked if anyone spoke the Ojibwe language in his family. *"Our grandparents would say things in Ojibwe that we didn't know what it meant. My dad spoke French and Ojibwe on occasion."*

He explained some of other the family traditional practices. *"While we are also here, we have a responsibility of living up to the name, the family tradition, not just Ojibwe, the family's tradition. That is to stand up and go out and work hard. Share what you get Take care of your kids, those kids are first. That's the facts of life, be a realist... Reality to us is we were not born into richness and power, the kind that either some people were born into or come into. We have our own power and wealth and values. And they are very tough because we had experiences like the boarding school, rheumatic fever and other things, poverty, death, suicide, all the things have visited our home, our families. But our tradition is to stand up to it and not give up... That's our tradition. We have to be strong about things. We are not defeatist, we're pacifists."*

Tim explained his philosophy regarding education and the problems many Native American families still face as a result of the infractions of the past. *"Good traditional teachers have helped me understand things. But what I have is the right to utilize all the knowledge I have no matter where it comes from. That could be from Germany or India, the Ojibwe or anywhere. I don't think that*

Ojibwe people were racist or segregationist. I also had a good relationship with our environment and everything in it. I think that's what it takes to be fully human... Things happened to our ancestors that devastated them. That was supposed to destroy us. It didn't totally destroy us, but it sure did a lot of damage. So now we have some of this dysfunction to deal with. We have had four to five hundred years of this kind of treatment. The dysfunctions that are rampant in our families, the addictions. We also have the external pushing and pulling, too. It is a very tough challenge. It's like asking a six-year-old in a boarding school who is dealing with disease and distress to understand. It was designed to really break you down. Make you into something different."

The interview was ended with a discussion about the tragedy their family was currently facing. His mother had a stroke. "The four oldest kids went to boarding school, now that we are going through this crisis, my mom had a stroke you know, the four of us aligned in a way that we say we want certain kind of treatment for our mother. The three youngest seem to differ from that. Not that they want anything worse or better. There is a split. I think part of it is there was an alliance built between the four of us."

Interview #8: Jennifer from St. Ignace

Jennifer was in her mid-sixties when I interviewed her. Missionaries influenced the upbringing of her father during his childhood. Jesuits lived in her father's home when he was a child. Jennifer's childhood was riddled with sexual abuse, physical abuse and neglect. Her father worked, but a lot of his paycheck was spent on alcohol. On more than one period in their lives, the family faced poverty. Another problem was the discrimination of the times. Her father could not claim his Ojibwe heritage in order to seek and maintain employment. His age was another factor. He was approximately fifty years old before he started his family. When he was about to pass away, he lay in his bed and speak the Ojibwe and French languages to himself.

Social workers placed her in the Holy Childhood boarding school with her older sister, because of the abuse and other circumstances that occurred in their home. Her brothers attended the same boarding school. Jennifer was six years old when she spent a year there. "We went to school as I refer to it as the school of hell... It was so huge.

Scared to death. The first thing they did was shave our hair off. I had beautiful brown hair and they shaved it off. They said it was because of lice... We wore dark black little pinafores, black stockings. We looked like we were from a concentration camp. We were just so pitiful."

"*We could smell the food, it was rotten. If you were sick and couldn't eat, they would punish you, you would have to sit there... We had to scrub. There was black marks from these shoes and there was these big long hallways... We used kerosene rags. I would just get so sick. You could hear those rosaries, and those shoes, they would go click, click, click... I remember there were a couple of nuns that were really nice. Especially the one in the kitchen... There was this one priest that befriended us when we went out and played. I learned to skip rope. I skipped and skipped and skipped when I was outside.*"

"*My parents never came. Not even an aunt or an uncle... We had a playroom. I would spend a lot of time gazing out the playroom window, because I could see. I would watch and surely today someone would come... As bad as it was at home, you still miss your parents and my aunt Helen. My sister and I would huddle in bed together.*"

"*When I wet the bed, she would help me so the nuns would not find out. Wash the sheets out and try to put them on the register and they wouldn't see the wet bed so I wouldn't get a beating. They took you in front of everybody, laid you across the bed and used a rubber hose. As young as you were when you wet the bed... I wasn't the only one but at the time I felt like I was the only one. I remember I watched how they treated the other children. You used to always hear like howling, they sounded like animals howling. Then I found out later that it was a dungeon that they had down below. It was solitary confinement... We were up at the crack of dawn, going to church. We went to church at noon. We went to church in the evening. Here's these people praising God and they are so mean. I got so many mixed messages. So confused.*"

Poverty led to childhood memories that were still carried into adulthood. "*Nobody knows the feeling of being hungry. No place to go and you are hungry. In the summertime, we stole from gardens. We raided people's gardens, and we had apples... We swiped potatoes. Other people fed us... We needed mittens to walk to school... my mother took an old coat and sewed us mittens. We had* these ugly mittens. We had to walk, these big old coats. We used to get clothes at the courthouse. They had a box that we could look through and get some clothes. You know, when I was a child, I might have been lacking a lot of things but outdoors and nature was my thing. Yeah, playing outside and being with my friends... We had the freedom to go... We are lucky we are alive today, some of the places we went. We just loved to go and explore. To climb places and go and explore. Just like heaven to us. My grandmother would make some of the most delicious cookies, they were big. It was like mincemeat. She was a fabulous baker and cook."

The boarding school experience and other childhood experiences have made an impact on her life as a whole. "I had trouble with abandonment and being alone and lonely. I never felt like this inner peace that you get. I always felt that there was something missing... Through my younger years and my teenage years, I was really, really lonely, even though I had friends. 'Cause I know that feeling of being in prison. Being cornered or trapped bothers me more. I'm claustrophobic in certain places. I can't go underground... I felt trapped when I was at school." She was faced with identity issues because of her gender and her race. Her father used to call them "useless girls" and her husband used to call her a "squaw." These circumstances angered her so much and she said it had an effect on her self-esteem.

Jennifer described her marriage to an alcoholic, and being medicated in the 1950s. They tranquilized women all the time back then. She said she discovered her Indian heritage and started attending sweat lodge ceremonies. She has learned her Ojibwe name and clan affiliation and has discovered an outlet, which was painting with watercolors. This discovery occurred after trying various other crafts and art activities. She has met with other people who have attended the Holy Childhood boarding school and have discussed their experiences. Jennifer said she found support in sharing her experiences with others who attended the Holy Childhood boarding school.

Interview #9: Diane from St. Ignace

Diane lived with her family on Mackinac Island when she was a child and was in her mid-fifties when I met her. Her father worked for Edison Sault Electric Company. Poverty was not an issue for this family. They had a lot of freedom to explore on the island, except their mother would not allow them to go near the docks or by the water. The older siblings cared for the younger ones and brought them along when they went out to play. They earned money by singing for the tourists who visited the island. As children, they would play house in the woods. They picked herbs and plants and made dishes out of leaves. She was asked how she knew which plants were safe to eat and she said they just knew. Diane was the second oldest of ten children in her family.

Diane was close to her grandmother, who passed away when she was only five. Her parents drank on the weekends but otherwise provided for them well. Diane did not know why her parents sent her and her siblings to the Holy Childhood boarding school. *"They were good parents. They were both alcoholics, weekend alcoholics. ... We had to listen to some awful fights... They took good care of us. Of course, they shipped us all off, too. He always made sure we had our bikes and there was always a horse around for us to ride."* But if her grandmother would have been alive, she would have never allowed her parents to send them to the boarding school. Diane attended the boarding school in Harbor Springs for approximately six years.

Her biggest complaint about her stay was the lack of peanut butter. *"We would think peanut butter was so plentiful that we would get it more often... if it was at a meal you would take that and scraped it to the corner of the bread... You wanted it to last as long as you could. We would go home... There would always be a couple of loaves of Bunny Bread and a couple of jars of peanut butter sitting on the table. There was homemade bread down there. We never ate that store-bought bread. You get tired of homemade bread... The nuns bread was always sweeter than ours... You would sneak that bread like crazy... There were nuns supervising everything. The nuns did most of the cooking. We didn't have to do that."*

Diane appreciated the fact the staff at the boarding school taught her how to sew, embroider and other things such as cleaning and maintenance. She was asked to compare her experience with the public school as opposed to the boarding school. *"I think it's a lot better because of the discipline."* She explained they would have races with her fellow students and whoever won the race would get a piece of candy. The races involved numbers and other learning tasks. *"You had an incentive to do it."* Diane enjoyed watching the movies and participating in the other fun activities. Part of her acceptance of the boarding school she related to the fact that she reminded the nuns her father was paying for them to attend. The other children who complained about attending the school were from poverty situations except for one. Her complaints about the problems she faced were less in number and severity than the other interviewees who attended the Holy Childhood boarding school.

Diane explained in some detail about the medical care provided by the staff at the school. *"Every night everybody lined up and if you had any complaints or anything, got a cold... you were given kerosene and sugar. If you needed a poultice, they had sticks... some Indian made them for that. And she would break you off a little piece. You would work it with your fingers until it was soft until they got to you and then they would put it under the gauze and put it where it was needed... After every holiday they would give you a pretty good meal. You had to line up and everybody would get Carters Little Liver Pills. They gave you this good meal and then they would give you pills to shit it out."*

Special jobs such as painting the walls in the rectory were assigned to her and a few other children. They were rewarded with treats such as ice cream. The children were taken on field trips to the Ramada Inn Hotel and they would play around the pool. Diane reported climbing the fire escapes. Cottages were located by the lake. The lake was near the school. She and her school friends would enter the cottages without permission during the night. *"There was a bunch of cottages around the lake. We would break into those cottages. If there was a piano someone would bang on the piano, and we would dance. We never did any damage though. We would put it all back when we got done. We would just have a ball in those old houses. And sometimes the boys would meet us out there. Down in a different direction, four or five of us would go off with boys. Just the fact that we could do it, you know."*

Her worst memory as a child was when her sister died. Her best memory involved her father bringing a horse home for the children to ride.

Diane was asked if she was involved with extended family members other than her grandmother. *"There were cousins, but we call them aunts. They were my mother's age. We used to go around there."* Then she addressed her anger to some degree. *"...I beat her up one time. I would have killed her if they didn't stop me. She beat up my little sister... I was a big bully."* She was not in contact with the children she went to school with on Mackinac Island, but she was and has continued to be involved with her family.

She explained living in Alaska. There was a girl who graduated from the Holy Childhood boarding school. *"I met her twenty-five years later in Fairbanks, Alaska. She came to my house with a friend of mine to use my telephone...And we hung out for two years..."* Her friendships during her stay at the boarding school were discussed further. *There was this family that were migrant workers and their folks would drop them off and they would go and pick at other places...They would come back and tell us all the stories about their experiences and ... was my age. She was the best storyteller. I remember 20,0000 Leagues Under the Sea and she came back and we would all sit around and she would tell that story. She could really narrate it without the book..."*

What were other positive experiences while at the boarding school? *"I remember in fifth or sixth grade, I was the one who got picked to paint the windows on the stores. I won the recruiting poster. Must have been during the war... In November she* (the nun) *would start making Christmas cookies. They were always Jesus, Mary and Joseph, the manger scene. We would paint them with egg whites and food coloring and stuff. Like the Twelve Days of Christmas... we would get these three cookies for breakfast... There was Roxy the taxi driver. She would take us to school and she would come and pick us up when it was time to come. She had the most wonderful car. I can still smell it today when I think about it. Those seats were so deep, and you would just sink away in it...It was a comfy and kind of cozy feeling when you think about it."*

Traditional practices such as language or songs were discussed. *"Sister ..., she was the little old Indian lady... She was one of the first ones that started Harbor Springs. When we first went there, she taught us to say the Lord's Prayer in Indian. But I couldn't remember a word of it now... There were no benefits to being Indian like there is now. Everybody's Indian... It was 1947 when we went..."*

She was asked if there was additional things she would like to share about the school. *"Scared. It was very scary. We didn't have any experiences with nuns before. We' never spent any time away from home... Most of the kids that went there didn't have much of a family life besides, anyways."* Diane shared many recollections about her boarding school experiences. Most appeared to be of a positive nature. The interview ended with Diane's explanation of the high school graduation she was going to attend that evening.

Individual Interview Analysis

Tables delineated the results for each individual interview participant. The tables were numbered in the order represented by the interview summaries listed in the oral historical accounts. Each table gave a horizontal and vertical representation for each individual interview participant. The horizontal axis denoted time periods. These were listed at the top of each table and were: 1) Epistemology of the family of origin; 2) Boarding school experience; and 3) Post-boarding school experience. Concerning epistemology of the family of origin, interview participants gave testimony of the nature of this to the best of their recollection. What were the central concepts they remembered such as poverty, involvement with friends and family, abandonment, and alcoholism. The vertical axis represented the themes described in the interview summaries.

Mt. Pleasant Boarding School

Interview One: Jeff from Haslett, MI

Epistemology of the Family of Origin	Boarding School Experience	Post Boarding School Experience
Poverty Alcoholism Lived on a Reservation Importance placed on Involvement with Family and Friends	Resistance to Authority Developed Alliances with Other Children and Adults Court Ordered to Attend the Boarding School Multigenerational Attendance of Boarding Schools or Missionary Training Explained Regimented Teaching Practices	Identity Confusion Institutionalization/ Materialism Importance placed on Involvement with Family and Friends

Interview Two: Doris from Sault Ste. Marie

Epistemology of the Family of Origin	Boarding School Experience	Post Boarding School Experience
Importance Placed on Involvement with Family and Friends Abandonment (Father's and Mother's death)	Importance placed on Involvement with Family and Friends Personal Choice to Send Child(ren) to the Boarding School Explained Regimented Teaching Practices Expressed Feelings of Loneliness and Abandonment (mother and father died)	Institutionalization/ Materialism Importance Placed on Involvement with Family and Friends

Interview Three: Fred from Sault Ste. Marie

Epistemology of the Family of Origin	Boarding School Experience	Post Boarding School Experience
Poverty	Developed Alliances with Other Children and Adults	Institutionalization/ Materialism
Importance Placed on Involvement with Family and Friends	Explained Regimented Teaching Practices	Traditional Cultural Practices
Traditional Cultural Practices	Parents' Personal Choice to Send Child(ren) to the Boarding School (i.e. poverty, large families, etc.)	Importance Placed on Involvement with Family and Friends
Ojibwe Language Forbidden or not Encouraged	Resistance to Authority	Continued Alliances with Those who Attended the Boarding Schools.
Abandonment (father moved to Detroit)		Regrets About Not Knowing the Ojibwe Language

Holy Childhood Boarding School

Interview Four: Kent from Sugar Island

Epistemology of the Family of Origin	Boarding School Experience	Post Boarding School Experience
Poverty

Importance Placed on Involvement with Family and Friends

Traditional Cultural Practices

Lived on a Reservation | Resistance towards Authority

Developed Alliances with Other Children and Adults

Aggression Towards Other Children and Adults

Stated Incidences of Harsh Discipline and Communication with Parents was Censored

Personal Choice to Send Children to the Boarding School (i.e. poverty; large families, etc.)

Ojibwe Language Forbidden at the Boarding School

Explained Regimented Teaching Practices | Identity Confusion

Fears and Phobias

Traditional Cultural Practices

Importance Placed on Involvement with Family and Friends

Resentments Toward Being Sent to the Boarding School

Continued Alliances with Those who Attended the Boarding School

Regrets About Not Knowing the Ojibwe Language |

Interview Five: Yulanda from Petoskey

Epistemology of the Family of Origin	Boarding School Experience	Post Boarding School Experience
Importance Placed on Involvement with Family and Friends

Traditional Cultural Practices

Abandonment (Mother left the family) | Resistance towards Authority

Developed Alliances with Other Children and Adults

Incidences of Harsh Discipline and Communication with Parents was Censored

Court Ordered to attend the Boarding School

Ojibwe Language Forbidden at the Boarding School

Explained Regimented Teaching Practices

Multigenerational Attendance of Boarding Schools

Importance Placed on Involvement with Family and Friends | Fears and Phobias

Traditional Cultural Practices

Importance Placed on Involvement with Family and Friends

Resentments Stated About Being Sent to the Boarding School

Continued Alliances with Those who Attended the Boarding School

Regrets About Not Knowing the Ojibwe Language

Institutionalization |

Interview Six: Brenda from St. Ignace

Epistemology of the Family of Origin	Boarding School Experience	Post Boarding School Experience
Importance Placed on Involvement with Family and Friends

Ojibwe Language was not Encouraged | Resistance to Authority

Developed Alliances with Other Children and Adults

Parents' Personal Choice to Send Children to the Boarding School

Multigenerational Attendance of Boarding Schools or Missionary Training

Mixed Messages About Religion

Incidences of Harsh Discipline and Communication with Parents was Censored | Importance Placed on Involvement with Family and Friends

Resentments Towards Upbringing by Parents

Continued Alliances with Those Who Attended the Boarding Schools

Resentments About Being Sent to the Boarding School |

Interview Seven: Tim from Sault Ste. Marie

Epistemology of the Family of Origin	Boarding School Experience	Post Boarding School Experience
Poverty	Incidences of Harsh Discipline and Communication with Parents was Censored	Fears and Phobias
Alcoholism		Traditional Cultural Practices
Domestic Violence	Personal Choice to Send Children to the Boarding School	
Importance Placed on Involvement with Family and Friends	Mixed Messages About Religion	Importance Placed on Involvement with Family and Friends
Traditional Cultural Practices	Expressed Feelings about Loneliness and Abandonment	Resentments About Being Sent to the Boarding School
Lived on a Reservation	Importance Placed on Involvement with Family and Friends	
		Continued Alliances with Those who Attended the Boarding School

Interview Eight: Jennifer from St. Ignace

Epistemology of the Family of Origin	Boarding School Experience	Post Boarding School Experience
Poverty

Alcoholism

Importance Placed on Involvement with Family and Friends

Abuse | Multigenerational Attendance of Boarding Schools

Incidences about Harsh Discipline

Alliances Developed with Children and Adults

Expressed Feelings about Abandonment and Loneliness Issues

Mixed Messages About Religion

Importance Placed on Involvement with Family and Friends

Court Ordered to Attend the Boarding School | Identity Confusion

Fears and Phobias

Traditional Cultural Practices

Importance Placed on Involvement with Family and Friends

Resentments About Being Sent to the Boarding School

Continued Alliances with Those Who Attended the Boarding School |

Interview Nine: Diane from St. Ignace

Epistemology of the Family of Origin	Boarding School Experience	Post Boarding School Experience
Alcoholism	Resistance To Authority	Resentments About Being Sent to the Boarding School
Domestic Violence	Developed Alliances with Other Children and Adults	
Importance Placed on Involvement with Family and Friends	Parents' Personal Choice to Send Children to the Boarding School	Importance placed on involvement with family and friends
	Explained Regimented Teaching Practices	
	Aggression Towards Other Children	Continued Alliances with Those Who Attended the Boarding Schools
	Importance Placed on Involvement with Family and Friends	

Summary of Results

The following tables delineated the three different time periods addressed during the interview sessions. These included: 1) The epistemology of family of origin; 2) boarding school experience; and 3) Post Boarding School experience. Themes presented more than one time in the interview summaries were referred to as major themes. Frequencies were tabulated to represent the number of people who expressed statements that indicated the themes applied to them. The respondents were separated by the boarding school they had attended (i.e., Holy Childhood and Mt. Pleasant). There were nine interview participants. Six attended the Holy Childhood boarding school and three attended the Mt. Pleasant boarding school.

Table Ten - Epistemology of the Family of Origin

Major Themes	Mt. Pleasant Boarding School	Holy Childhood Boarding School	Themes Not Evident
Poverty	Two	Three	Four
Ojibwe Language Not Encouraged or Forbidden	One	Four	Four
Traditional Cultural Practices	One	Three	Five
Alcoholism	One	Three	Five
Lived on a Reservation	One	Two	Six
Abandonment	Two	One	Six
Domestic Violence	None	Two	Seven

Table Eleven - Boarding School Experience

Major Themes	Mt. Pleasant Boarding School	Holy Childhood Boarding School	Themes Not Evident
Developed Alliances with Children and Adults	One	Five	Three
Importance Placed on Involvement with Family and Friends	One	Four	Four
Regimented Teaching and Monitoring Practices	Three	Three	Three
Personal Choice to Send Child (ren) to the Boarding Schools	Two	Four	Three
Resistance to Authority	Two	Four	Three
Multigenerational Attendance of Boarding Schools	One	Three	Five
Incidences of Harsh Discipline and Communication with Parents was Censored	None	Four	Five
Mixed Messages About Religion	None	Three	Six
Court Ordered or Ordered by Social Services to Attend the Boarding Schools	One	Two	Six
Expressed Feelings of Abandonment	One	Two	Six
Aggression Towards Other Children	None	Two	Seven
Ojibwe Language Forbidden at School	None	Two	Seven

Table Twelve - Post Boarding School Experience

Major Themes	Mt. Pleasant Boarding School	Holy Childhood Boarding School	Themes Not Evident
Importance Placed on Involvement with Family and Friends	Three	Six	None
Continued Alliances with Those Who Attended the Boarding Schools	Three	Five	One
Resentments About Being Sent to the Boarding School	None	Six	Three
Traditional Cultural Practices	One	Four	Four
Fears and Phobias	None	Five	Four
Regrets About Not Knowing the Ojibwe Language	One	Five	Two
Identity Confusion	One	Two	Six
Institutionalization/ Materialism	Three	None	Six
Institutionalization/ Disciplined Behaviors	One	Six	Two

Chapter 5 – Discussion

The study involved the examination of potential factors that explained the perseverance of Native American people in regard to the exhibited strengths of the individuals who were interviewed and the problems they continue to face. One of the goals of this project was to compare the experiences of those who attended a federal and missionary boarding school covered by this study. Another goal was to seek information about the possible aftereffects of the boarding school experience. Three periods of time were delineated by this project. The interview participants portrayed both positive and negative recollections that explained the rationale behind the perceived resilience and difficulties still being faced by Native Americans.

Various areas were explored such as importance placed on involvement with family and friends and other sources of support which aided in their resilience. The boarding school experiences of these individuals happened to be both positive and negative in nature ranging from harsh treatment to the building of alliances. The possible aftereffects included, but are not limited to, their resentments towards being sent to the boarding schools, fears and phobias, inability to speak the Ojibwe language, and identity confusion. The strengths and problems that surfaced for these individuals were delineated by the following paragraphs. An explanation was given which may offer insight to how these factors were associated with their family of origin and their boarding school experience. The first topic to be discussed was the importance placed on involvement with family and friends.

Importance Placed on Involvement with Family and Friends

All of the interviewees placed importance on involvement with family and friends during their childhood and into their adulthood. These individuals gave examples of activities they participated in with family and friends such as the importance placed on attending community gatherings. The families shared any extra food they had with anyone who needed it. Harmless pranks were one of the ways of providing entertainment for one another. Humor continued to be a significant aspect for some of these individuals.

Grandparents played a vital role with many Native American families. They provided supervision, care, and guidance for their grandchildren. Kent said he spent more time with his grandparents when he was not at the boarding school than he did with his parents. Another said he went back and forth from his grandmother to his mother's home to live when he was a child. Siblings and other family members such as aunts and uncles provided protection for one another and provided food and other necessities. Jennifer and Tim said their families have suffered hardships such as suicide, depression, and poverty, but have faced these struggles together. I discovered these people found comfort and support in these relationships.

Native American people seek out other Native American people through various events such as powwows, sweat lodge ceremonies, feast meals and other social gatherings. These activities enhanced their sense of belonging. Fred told about his family's excursion to the Strongs area to pick blueberries with family members and friends. They set up camp and stayed in the area for almost the entire summer. The same person and others explained other positive family experiences as children and adults. These events oftentimes involved music and dancing. One of the interviewees relayed fond memories of singing in the glee club at school and another dancing and singing on stage at the Mt. Pleasant boarding school. Other cherished memories were playing and exploring outside with their friends and siblings, playing sports, hunting and fishing, reading, watching movies at the boarding school and the local movie theater, listening to the elders tell stories and other activities. A feeling of connection served as a way they managed to cope and help others.

Traditional Cultural Practices

Grandparents, considered prominent members of tribal families and communities, gave their grandchildren special gifts and experiences. One interview participant shared his experiences about cooking with his grandparents. They cooked the traditional way by burying the vegetables in the ground under the fire and the meat was cooked in a cast iron pot over the fire. Kent told a legend during the interview associated with this cultural practice. Stories were told around campfires. Yulanda reported she visited an elder's home and listened to some of the stories and/or legends. This individual told two legends associated with the first porcupine. (Refer to appendix 1). Legends were utilized to provide entertainment and lessons and was an important cultural tradition. The same individuals, who were exposed to the traditional cultural practices when they were children, still carried out some of the same cultural traditions in their present lives such as attending powwows and telling legends. Their continued interest concerning their traditional cultural practices assisted them with hanging onto a portion or their entire identity as a Native American person.

Ojibwe Language (Anishaanabemowin)

Interview participants made reference to not knowing the Ojibwe language. They said they regret not learning the language as children. Some of the participants said their parents did not want to teach them the language to protect them. If they spoke the language, they could receive harsh treatment at the boarding schools. Fred said he ran the other way when he heard his family and extended family members speaking the language. Kent and Yulanda reported that speaking the Ojibwe language was forbidden at the boarding school. Yulanda witnessed a girl being punished for speaking the language and another stated it was an unspoken rule. Barriers to learning the Ojibwe language have existed throughout the three time periods delineated by this project. History and culture is inherent in language. Learning the native language denoted learning the same history and culture of their parents, relatives, and multiple generations (Littlefield, 2001).

Lived on a Reservation

Three interview participants informed me they had resided on a reservation when they were children. Living on a reservation was associated with poverty and other problems the families faced. All three of these families moved off the reservation to seek employment. The land in which the reservation was on was not suitable for agriculture and wild game was not available in quantities to provide sustenance for the people living on the reservation. This information correlated with some of the materials reviewed for the literature review.

Multigenerational Attendance of Boarding Schools

Another factor to consider was four of the individuals interviewed said their parents and other extended family members attended either the Holy Childhood or Mt. Pleasant boarding schools and one had a parent who was influenced by the Jesuits. An intergenerational form of assimilation with either religion or education had already occurred with these families.

Alcoholism

Four interview participants reported their families to have been plagued with alcoholism, which caused many problems, especially neglect. A couple of their parents did not provide food and clothing for their families because money was being spent on alcohol. One common denominator existed in regard to addictive behaviors. Addictions were used to achieve detachment from feelings. Detachment lessens the feelings of pain (Steffen, 1999).

Domestic Violence

Tim and Diane, who attended the Holy Childhood boarding school, indicated domestic violence was a problem their families of origin faced. One stated her parents would have some awful fights and another reported even if the domestic violence incidences were occurring, home was still a better place than the boarding school. The origins of domestic violence concerning Native Americans was not explored during this study. Assimilation and other forms of oppression may have caused this problem. During the traditional period for Native Americans, women were highly respected.

Poverty

Five of the interview participants made reference to their families suffering from poverty. Jennifer stated she often experienced hunger as a child and would raid gardens to obtain food. Poverty often forced parents to focus primarily on the day-to-day survival while other important aspects of the family were neglected. Poverty generated feelings of hostility towards people in positions of authority. Tribal people were forced onto reservations without being provided a means of providing subsistence for their families. This dilemma may have led them down a bumpy road of frustration, anger and resentments (Horejsi, et al., 1991). The disruption of the cultural development by being removed from their family of origin and the loss of family roles such as the provider role were phenomena delineated by the process of ethnostress. Ethnostress was a disruption of the development of cultural beliefs and personal identity due to acts of oppression.

An interesting point to note was by Diane, who said she was treated with more respect by the employees at the Holy Childhood boarding school because she reminded the nuns that her father paid for them to attend the school. Poverty was not an issue for two interview participants who did not state an issue about the abuse that occurred at the Holy Childhood boarding school. Poverty did not appear to be an issue for the interview participants during the time the interviews were conducted.

Court Ordered/Parents' Personal Choice to Send Child(ren) to the Boarding School

Three of the interview participants were court ordered to attend the boarding schools and six were sent due to personal choice of the parents. Jennifer and Yulanda reported child abuse and neglect were reasons for being sent to the school. One participant reported she and her siblings were abandoned by the babysitters left in charge of them. Their home was without heat and food. The other stated that alcoholism, child abuse and poverty were reasons why she was placed in the school with her sister. Alcoholism and poverty were the reasons given by another participant who was court ordered to attend the boarding school. Parents' personal choice was in reference to the economic status of the families at the time they were sent to the boarding schools for three of the interview participants. They were sent because of poverty and large families. Their parents had difficulty feeding and clothing all of their children.

Doris said her mother had difficulty raising her on her own since the death of her father. However, her mother went to visit her while she was attending the boarding school and brought her gifts. Yulanda, who attended the Holy Childhood boarding school, said her father had attended the same boarding school and he wanted his children to have the same opportunity he had. Another mentioned she did not know why her parents sent her to the school. Poverty was not an issue for the last three participants mentioned in this section. No matter what the reason was for the attendance at the boarding schools, the interview participants who attended the Holy Childhood Boarding School resented being sent there.

Aggression Toward Other Children

Three of the interview participants indicated they demonstrated acts of aggression when they were children and during their adolescent years. Acts of aggression were modeled by the staff at the Holy Childhood boarding school through the harsh types of discipline, in their homes and by their peers. People become products of their environments (Bandura, 1973).

Harsh Discipline and Censored Communication/Fears and Phobias

The same number of interview participants, who attended the Holy Childhood boarding school, who accounted for incidences that involved harsh discipline, also reported they have fears and/or phobias. Five expressed their fear of the dark and one had a fear of numbers and math. Kent reported he was forced to sit at the bottom of the stairs in the basement in the dark. He always had a fear of the basement while attending the boarding school. He continued to have difficulty going outside in the dark. Tim reported they instilled a fear of the devil in him. Today, he has a fear of the dark. Jennifer thought she heard children screaming during the night and she thought there was a dungeon in the basement where children were locked up as a form of punishment. She reported having a fear of the dark.

Yulanda said she had refused employment promotions because they required her to work with budgets. Her hair happened to be thinner on one side of her head because the hair was pulled out when she had difficulty doing math problems while she attended the Holy

Childhood boarding school. Her head was also slammed into the wall or blackboard if she didn't know how to do a math problem. Tim and Jennifer reported severe infractions for bedwetting. One was beaten with a rubber hose in front of her peers and another was made to wear the sheets with urine on them in front of his peers.

On more than one occasion, it was mentioned the correspondence that was sent to their parents was censored by the nuns at the Holy Childhood Boarding School. Their letters could only consist of special activities such as field trips and going for walks. The children could not tell their parents about the abuse and other inappropriate behaviors. The letters were returned to them to make the requested changes before they were sent to their parents. It appeared that abuse was linked to the phobias and fears the children developed and they could not report the incidences to their parents.

Harsh treatment and censored communication caused a whole host of problems such as sense of hopelessness. The children had no one to turn to for protection, which can also lead to feelings of abandonment. The long-lasting devastation stemming from the horrible abuse led to the development of fears and phobias for many of the boarding school children.

Mixed Messages About Religion

Another topic that caused problems for the children who attended the Holy Childhood Boarding School was the mixed messages about religion. I concluded that most of the nuns and priests did not establish credibility with the children because these preachers of the gospel also appeared to break a lot of the rules stated in the ten commandments. It was reported that one of the nuns asked the children to lie about the breaking of a car window. The nuns beat and humiliated the children all in the name of the Lord. The nuns and priests, according to one report, were participating in immoral acts during holidays such as Christmas and Easter. The mixed messages portrayed by the nuns and priests added to their feelings of identity confusion and cultural disruption.

Expressed Feelings of Abandonment

Doris said both of her parents had died. Yulanda and Fred said one of their parents left the family home when they were children.

These parents had little to no involvement with their upbringing. Jennifer and Tim stated that they'd missed their siblings and other family members when they were attending the boarding school. Jennifer said she would stare out the window waiting for someone from her family to visit her. Being away from family caused a whole host of problems for children, especially when forced to be in harsh environments.

Regimented Teaching and Monitoring Practices at the Boarding Schools

The majority of the interview participants described the regimented teaching and monitoring practices at the boarding schools. They explained most of the transition periods between activities involved marching and standing in lines. The lines were from the oldest to the youngest boarders and girls and boys were segregated. A strict schedule and rules were developed for daily activities. Those not following the rules were disciplined.

Institutionalization/Materialism

The identification and acceptance of the mainstreaming of Native Americans into the European American Culture was observed. The ones who attended the Mt. Pleasant boarding school focused on their adult children's employment positions and the material objects their children possessed such as their nice cars and homes. These interview participants readily accepted the values promoted at the boarding school. The work ethics that were promoted were associated with hard work and the acquisition of material goods. They were conditioned to accept the values and norms of the European Americans such as materialism.

Institutionalization/Disciplined Behaviors

Institutionalization meant the adaptation of the regimented practices, their inability to communicate with others and once released from the institution they felt they did not belong with their family of origin due to their long absence and they acted differently. They did not fit in at the high school they attended. Many ended up in abusive relationships and they dealt with unwanted pregnancies.

For example, Yulanda, who attended the Holy Childhood boarding school, said her high school days were the loneliest days in her life. She did not know how to communicate with her classmates and talk about the normal topics teenagers talk about. The boarding school was noted as taking one's ability to think for themselves away from those who attended. She walked stiffly through the halls and did not participate in classroom discussions. Her grades were poor in high school because classroom participation was considered a substantial part of the grade. Talking was not allowed at the Holy Childhood boarding school during the scheduled class time or other parts of the day such as meal time.

Yulanda explained she completed household tasks in somewhat of the same scheduled regimented routine she adopted from the boarding school experience. For example, she did her laundry every Saturday as they did at the boarding school. One of the interview participants reported when he was in the army, they asked him if he went to West Point because of his marching abilities. The time in which they spent in these institutions varied from one to seven years. These individuals were highly trained to follow orders and did not establish the ability to think for themselves.

Developed Alliances with Other Children and Adults

Alliances were built in the boarding schools and some of these alliances continued into adulthood. Two-thirds of the people interviewed described a connection they felt with those who attended the same boarding school as they did. These alliances were explained in some of the literature resources and this phenomenon was reiterated during the interviews.

These alliances provided a multitude of benefits ranging from a form of communication to support. Yulanda relayed there was a secret language that existed which was comprised of eye and finger movements. She would be standing at the blackboard trying to complete a math problem and she would hear a quiet hissing sound or a tap of a pencil. These acts symbolized the support her peers were giving her while she was struggling to complete a task. The same person told about an incident when she was beaten and sent to bed without supper and a peer tried to sneak her food. These alliances were aligned with the various forms of resistance and resilience demonstrated by several boarding school students (Littlefield, 1989).

Resistance to Authority

Numerous reports indicated demonstrations of resistance to authority. These acts of resistance included the tearing of their stockings and throwing back their heads far enough so their hats fell off in church. Brenda stated they would do this in unison. Yulanda indicated she would not cry no matter what kind of abuse they inflicted on her. She waited until she was alone in her bed before she cried. Another reported sneaking out with his friends and going fishing or sneaking into town to steal items from a local store. Jeff reported breaking into cabins at night.

A subculture was created with those who attended these boarding schools. The subculture phenomena developed within the larger context (Bandura, 1973). Two entities existed within this subculture of the boarding school. These consisted of the ones in authority and the ones who were expected to be submissive. The ones expected to be submissive fought desperately to hold onto their sense of autonomy (Littlefield, 1989).

Identity Confusion

Evidence of identity confusion surfaced during the analysis of the data collected from the interviews. Yulanda and Kent, who attended the Holy Childhood boarding school, and one participant, who attended the Mt. Pleasant boarding school, indicated they struggled with their identity as a Native American person. Jeff on more than one occasion commented that he considered himself lucky to have been raised by "white people." This same person said Native American people must marry other Native American people. He was listed as being faced with identity confusion because on more than one occasion he contradicted himself in a similar manner.

Kent stated he felt like he was given somebody else's culture. He was making an attempt to learn about his cultural background. Every day he learned an Ojibwe word. He attended ceremonies such as feast meals and explained the water drum ceremony he had recently attended. Jennifer said she was not at peace until she begin practicing traditional cultural activities such as sweat lodge ceremonies and had found her medium with watercolors.

Shame was linked to the some of the problems being faced by the persons interviewed. One of the interview participants relayed he was ashamed to be a Native American person. Childhood experiences have also led to long-lasting effects of one's psychological wellbeing. The feelings of shame were derived from the feelings of powerlessness. However, while being placed in that position of powerlessness the child oftentimes experienced feelings of being inadequate and unworthy. These feelings may place the adult in a position void of personal power and promote feelings and thoughts of predicted failure concerning the outcomes of future endeavors.

Resentments Stated About Being Sent to the Boarding School

All of the interview participants who had attended the Holy Childhood boarding school said they disliked their boarding school experience and expressed anger at being sent to the boarding school. They explained the incidents that involved harsh discipline, the loneliness they felt for their families, the distasteful food, and the vast amount of work they had to do to assist with the maintenance of the boarding school. The interview participant who portrayed more positive details about her boarding school experience also said if her grandmother would have been alive she would not have been sent to the boarding school.

None of the interview participants who attended the Mt. Pleasant boarding school indicated they had regrets about attending there. They were quick to relay the positive experiences about the boarding school. They expressed their appreciation about the food, the structure, hygiene practices and instruction. These interview participants said their attendance at the boarding school was in their best interest.

The reports from individuals who attended the two institutions varied in areas such as harsh treatment, fears and phobias, mixed messages about religion, adaptation of materialism, aggression and the importance of traditional cultural practices. The ones who attended the Mt. Pleasant Boarding School did not say they resented being sent to the school, while all six who attended the Holy Childhood Boarding School resented being sent there. Could the absence of harsh treatment or other factors cause the people who attended the Mt. Pleasant boarding school to not resent being sent to the institution?

Summary of Discussion

As the researcher, I explained the reasons associated with perceived perseverance and possible aftereffects of the boarding school experience. The rationale behind the perseverance included the importance of the involvement with friends and extended family members and traditional cultural practices. The alliances built in the boarding school and during their childhood and adulthood provided a source of support for the interview participants. The activities linked to forms of resistance and alliances aided in their feelings of belonging and gave them the strength to survive the highly structured, oppressive and domineering atmosphere of the boarding schools. Their association with the Native American culture also provided them with a clarification of their Native American identity.

I provided information about the negative aftereffects, which included, but were not limited to, identity confusion, the personal problems some of the individuals still suffer such as their fears and phobias and shame, institutionalization, and resentments towards the boarding school experience, Nobody has ever been known to be completely assimilated (Fixico, 2000). A multitude of Native Americans have continued to participate in traditional cultural practices of the past. Native American people have had to learn to live in two worlds.

Implications for Further Research

Limitations for this study included the fact this was a master's thesis. This type of research is limited to a short time period to complete the study. Qualitative data analysis was a fundamental methodology for the interpretation of research, but it did have certain limitations. Words, as opposed to numbers, can have multiple meanings. Another point to consider was only one researcher interpreted the data. Thus, the analysis of the data was based solely on my points of reference. I noted that the small sample that was selected to be a part of this project was another limitation. An imbalance occurred between the number of interview participants selected who attended these institutions. The results of this study cannot be attributed to all Native American people who attended boarding schools. Also, the age of some of the interview participants may have hindered their ability to recall the events concerning while attending the boarding school.

Other areas existed that could have been improved to add more to the accuracy and amount of the data collection. Some of the problems faced with this project included that I did not explore the religious practices to the point in which that area needed to be explored with the interview participants who attended the Mt. Pleasant boarding school. Literature about the Holy Childhood boarding school was practically nonexistent. A few newspaper articles existed and there were other materials that were in print but not accessible to me. Research materials that covered federal boarding schools in general were used to get a better understanding of the Mt. Pleasant Boarding School. I uncovered areas which may require future exploration.

Additional Questions for Future Studies

1. Were children given preferential treatment if their families were thought to have a higher socioeconomic status?

2. Did the interview participants inform the researcher about most of the significant problems their families were facing such as alcoholism and domestic violence?

3. What similarities and differences existed between the teaching practices of both the boarding schools and public schools during the boarding school era?

4. Did the discipline have a tendency to be harsher at the missionary boarding schools than at the federal boarding schools throughout the United States and Canada?

5. Are the findings related to the fears and/or phobias idiosyncratic to these individuals or to other individuals who received harsh treatment at the boarding schools?

6. Was the process of assimilation similar for all boarding school students from various tribes?

Chapter 6 – Implications of the Study

The results of this study give a better understanding about the aftereffects of the boarding school experience. The study covered the differentiation between experiences for those who attended the Mt. Pleasant and Holy Childhood boarding schools. Similarities and differences did exist according to this study. The individuals' recollections from their boarding school experiences were both negative and positive in nature. The Native American people who were interviewed, their families of origin, and their ancestors have survived generations of oppression such as the boarding school phenomena. They have not come through these horrible situations unscathed. The boarding school approach to assimilation was monumental in the destruction of the Native American culture. As a result, their sense of identity was profoundly affected. However, they have managed to adapt and work towards self-determination. Many Native American people have accomplished these goals by learning how to cope and survive in two different worlds.

Phobias and fears and other serious problems have continued to exist for those who attended the Holy Childhood boarding school. The programs that provide social services have not addressed these issues adequately, so many Native American people continue to suffer. However, the interview participants were not plagued with poverty. A variety of inner strengths appeared to provide a source of support for them, more so than outside entities such as social service programs.

The European American values practiced and explained in this study went against the main goals of the National Association of Social Worker Code of Ethics. The boarding school philosophy was not founded on the grounds of providing fairness and equity for Native American people. Areas that did not cover the rights of the families, included but were not limited to informed consent, cultural competence and social diversity, sexual relationships and physical contact, respect for worth and dignity of individuals, and the promotion of self-determination.

I accomplished a personal goal for myself. As a social worker, a basic understanding did exist that led to the belief that the boarding school experience did have a long-lasting negative effect on Native Americans. Associations existed between the experiences of those who were interviewed and my family and personal history. I uncovered a lot of information about the history of the Native Americans and in turn learned more about who I was as an individual. I struggled with my identity as a Native American person while trying to fit into two worlds. Meanwhile, personal strength has been gained as a result of these adversities. Future endeavors with providing social work services to Native American people will hopefully be enhanced given this insight. The following information covers the implications for social work practice at the micro, mezzo, and macro levels.

Implications for Social Work Practice: (Individual and Family, Community and National Perspectives)

Seven Generations

Look behind you. See your sons and your daughters. They are your future. Look farther and see your sons' and daughters' children and their children's children even unto the seventh generation. That's the way we were taught. Think about it—you yourself as a seventh generation.

Leon Sheandoah, Onondagan Elder
American Indian

Individual and Family Perspective

A multicultural view of today's Native American families would reveal a wide array of traditional values with a combination of current views and values. Each individual needed to be considered unique with a distinct worldview. The issues of the past concerning boarding schools may have had a contextual impact on individuals and their families. A culturally sensitive approach was recommended to be developed to address these issues. The approach may include a form of questioning that will help the clients define the difficulties they may be experiencing as a result of the past abuse they or their parents have suffered and address the strengths endemic in existence within their social context.

Other areas were recommended to be covered in order to meet the specific needs of Native American people. Social workers, who have worked with specific Native American populations, need to learn about the tribal history, value systems, tribal court systems, tribal family structures, tribal parenting styles, tribal community resources, contemporary child welfare issues that the community has been facing, and have knowledge about the various class and gender issues (Goodluck, 1993).

Social workers must be trained in communication skills and have the ability to obtain positive factors about individuals, and their environmental context. They need to be able to develop holistic studies about the people who may be in need of services. In addition, social workers need to have skills and/or knowledge in the areas of traditional healing practices, contemporary practice techniques, cross-cultural situations and empowerment techniques or have knowledge about where to direct clients for these services. The social workers repertoire needs to include certain values. These values include humanistic ethos, self-determination, confidentiality, respect for the worth and dignity of individuals, and respect and understanding of cultural differences (Goodluck, 1993). Tribal people and families need to be in control of their own treatment.

The healing process needs to be ongoing and lifelong. Clients and social workers need to work collaboratively toward termination of treatment. This determination shall be based on whether the client has enough understandable and conducive information to support and sustain their positive growth within the personal, family and community contextual units (Nabigon and Mawhiney, 1996).

Psychologists have developed a term that define the aftereffects of the boarding schools experience, which is "residential-school syndrome." Native American people have been exhibiting a distinct set of symptoms. This syndrome had been linked to the grief cycle that a person has gone through after the loss of a close relative. However, instead of losing someone close to them, the Native American people have lost a culture; something they were born with. This was a part of their soul, and it was obliterated by the missionaries and teachers (Taylor, 1995). Alcoholism, domestic violence, child abuse and neglect and the other social ills faced by Native Americans need to be considered symptoms of the boarding school experience (Taylor, 1995).

Community Perspective
The Human Family

O Great Spirit who made all races, look kindly upon the whole human family, and take away the arrogance and hatred that separates us from our brothers.

-Cherokee Prayer
American Indian

An approach may include educating the Native American people and general population about the aftereffects of the boarding school experience. Service providers need to look at the real reasons behind the problems still being faced by Native American people and look for new ways to meet this challenge. Social workers need to work collaboratively with clients for the attainment of personal and collective community social goals. Tribal community members need to be contacted to provide leadership for the accomplishment of the goals (Lee, 1996). A community healing process needed to be developed to address the unique needs of the community as a whole (Antone, et al., 1986).

The community healing process could begin with the development of community organizing. This may include individual relations, group effort, leadership, learning, short and long-range goals. Maintenance must be conducted once a community has regained control of its function. Part of the maintenance must include the education of the children, who will be providing the guidance and supervision for the future of the community. Progress made toward community goals needs to be monitored on an ongoing basis. The group recounts the collective history that has brought them together. The principles of the struggle must be maintained, and change may only occur if greater efficiency and effectiveness of those principles will be achieved. The group needs to welcome newcomers and integrate them into the group. Each person in the community must be empowered and given the personal power to be a part of the process of community healing and the maintenance of the process (Antone, et al., 1986).

National Perspective

Systems may not be influenced from inside forces, but outside pressures may provide the necessary influence. Many tribal members have sued the churches in Canada due to the abuse that incurred at the boarding schools (Bandura, 1973). Influential Canadians would be a good source of support in regard to changing policies for the benefit of Native Americans in the U.S., since efforts have been taken to address the aftereffects of the residential schools in Canada. Efforts to instill positive change can be met with successful outcomes if they support the majority beliefs. Enterprises that create jobs and services have flourished under the majority preferences, oftentimes at the expense of minorities. Eventually, there can be very long-lasting benefits to all if everyone's needs were considered. It would be important to get the key players to join in on the crusade to make attempts at developing new policies that will be of benefit to all.

Perspectives and life experiences of the dominant European American culture must be carefully examined. An active, political resistance needs to work against the material ideals of these perspectives and experiences. A developed understanding must be established with a rational, educated, and systematic approach in mind (Welton, 1997). One of the main goals of the assimilation process was to limit and choose the knowledge Native Americans obtained. The dominant culture wanted to keep Native Americans in the dark. They have succeeded to some degree. However, a voice needed to be given to the opposition of oppression (Hundleby, 1997).

Another point to be explored is the learning process at the elementary and high school levels. The facts were that schools were not conducive to their culture. National policies need to be implemented that address the special needs of Native American children. The European American culture often demonstrated a chosen form of ignorance and disinterest in the consequences of the faulty educational system. Hence, a large number of Native American children continued to be dropouts or push outs. Native American people must be a part of the development of all academic processes which involved Native American people including policy development (Sanchez and Stuckey, 1999).

The first order of business was for the European American culture to begin a process of developing an understanding of the Native

American culture. The second order of business was to address the inappropriate forms of instruction that was being provided to Native American students. Where in the history and social studies curriculum was the truth portrayed about Native Americans or history in general? To explain further, government-issued textbooks were used to commit cultural genocide. This concept continued to exist and has created much controversy. Native Americans must be a part of the development of all academic processes involving Native Americans, including policy development. It has been questioned if universal examinations such as the Scholastic Aptitude Test or the state Michigan Educational Assessment Program (MEAP) testing have replaced the beatings and public humiliation (Sanchez and Stuckey, 1999). These tests also ignore the specialized needs of Native American children.

Native Americans can and should direct the future of historical research involving Native Americans. The use of oral tradition, oral history, and the analysis of Native American languages would be ways of accomplishing the establishment of the true historical facts. The main goal involved an understanding of the history of the Native American population and not stereotype this group as a whole which can be accomplished by obtaining in-depth oral histories through the ethnographic process. The European American documents such as archives need to be examined for their authenticity. First and foremost, Native Americans need to be enlisted as consultants and be considered experts when it comes to the education of Native American students (Sanchez and Stuckey, 1999). The population as a whole in this country could learn from the past mistakes portrayed in this study and move forward with a more supportive environment.

Chapter 7 – Measuring the Impacts

Depression and Suicide:

Native American suicide rates have been 1.6 times greater than the national average. The suicide death rate for Native American male youth is 2.5 times greater than non-Native peers. The Indian Health Services (IHS) reported some of the social, educational and cultural issues associated with the high suicide rates: economic opportunity, access to educational alternatives, community and family breakdown and stigma. Depression was considered one of the most prominent underlying causes of suicide (U.S. Commission on Civil Rights, 2018).

Alcohol and Substance Abuse

Alcohol and substance abuse ranked as one of the most serious public health issues for Native Americans. The 2010 National Survey on Drug Use and Health reported that Native Americans required treatment for alcohol and drug abuse almost twice the national average (18.0 percent vs. 9.6 percent). The drug-related death rate for Native Americans was 1.8 times greater than the rate of all races nationwide. An added problem included the health disparities of alcohol and drug abuse such as high rates of mortality due to liver disease, unintentional injury and suicide (U.S. Commission on Civil Rights, 2018).

Health Disparities

Native Americans represented the highest rate of diagnosed diabetes in the nation. Approximately 16% of the Native population has been diagnosed with diabetes. The life expectancy for Native Americans was less than five years than other Americans.

Approximately, 55% of tribal people relied on the Indian Health Service for their medical and dental needs, however, the Indian Health Care Improvement Act only met approximately 60% of their health needs. The Indian Health Service was crisis-driven which led to a wide gap with providing adequate and preventative services for many Native Americans on the reservations. Pharmacies and doctors' offices beyond hospital services were scarce in some communities (Partnership with Native Americans, 2015).

The shift from a traditional way of life toward a Western lifestyle had drastically impacted the health and welfare of the indigenous and led to a terrible epidemic of chronic diseases such as diabetes, heart disease, tuberculosis, and cancer. The statistics have been alarming.

- Heart disease was the leading cause of death for American Indians.
- Due to the link between heart disease, diabetes, poverty, and quality of nutrition and health care, 36% of Natives with heart disease will die before age 65 compared to other Americans.
- American Indians were more likely to die from a variety of causes:
  - 177% more likely to die from diabetes.
  - 500% more likely to die from tuberculosis.
  - 82% more likely to die from suicide.
- Cancer rates and difficulties related to cancer treatment were higher than for other Americans.
- Infant death rates were 60% higher than for the white population (Partnership with Native Americans, 2015, para. 9).

Transportation

Transportation infrastructure served as a critical component for tribal governments and Native American citizens and was associated with the economic development of Indian people. The National Tribal Transportation Facility Inventory report revealed there are approximately 161,00 miles of existing roads in Indian country that were eligible for federal funding. 13,650 miles of roads and trails were owned and maintained by Indian tribes (93 percent were unpaved) and 29,400 miles of roads owned by the Bureau of Indian Affairs (BIA) (75 percent are unpaved). The aforementioned roads were mostly undeveloped, unsafe and poorly maintained (U.S. Commission on Civil Rights, 2018).

Education Disparities

According to the National Assessment of Educational Progress (NAEP) report, Native American students scored lower in every category annually. Grade four Native American students scored 69% in 2015 in math. The target level is 74% and all students scored 82%. At the eighth-grade level they scored 55%, the target was 63% and all students scored 71% in 2015. Lack of funding does not apply to the poor scores. NAEP scores involved basic reading level had demonstrated similar results. At fourth-grade level in 2015 Native American students scored 52%, the target level was 58% and actual all students scored 69%. At eighth-grade level during the same year, Native American students scored 63%, the target level was set at 69% and the actual all students scored at 76% (U.S. Commission on Civil Rights, 2018).

Native Americans have faced centuries of discrimination and heinous acts of genocide. The crippling effect of the continuous abuse had been a multitude of education, health and economic disparities. Alcohol was heavily introduced during the fur trading days by the European fur traders as a cheap commodity in exchange for the furs that Native Americans provided to them. The Indian people began to rely on alcohol to dull the pain of losing their land and way of life to the Anglo-invaders. Their traditional culture did not consist of a market economy and the over hunting of animals. They had respect for land and its resources that the Creator had provided for them.

Appendix 1 – Legends

The First Porcupine

Storytelling and/or the telling of legends was a way of teaching children about the history of Native American people and was also a method for instilling valuable lessons. Yulanda, an interview participant, told two legends about the first porcupine during the interview session. The first delineated how quills were given as protection and the other legend depicted a lesson about inappropriate behaviors.

First Legend

"One of the stories I remember is how we got porcupines. A long time ago porcupine was like humans. He had really soft skin. They still ate the same things. They ate greens and tree buds and things like that. They would climb trees to get away from the wild animals. One day this porcupine was out gathering in the woods. He was out in the field, the edge there and he was eating and across the field comes a great big wolf. So, he gets in the top of a tree as far as he could get so the wolf could not reach him. So, the wolf goes away."

"He is in that same field again and a bear comes across, growling and growling at him. The porcupine runs and climbs the tree, and the bear can't reach and the bear is trying to reach up and try to grab him. The porcupine is safe."

"So he goes away and the porcupine climbs back down and he wants to get something to eat so he is out in the field and he is eating. He's under a hawthorn bush eating the berries that are on the ground and he keeps eating. And the thorns are picking him in the back and hurt him. And he gets this idea. So, he gets these branches and ties them in a ball and crawls underneath the bush and then he goes out. Then there's a wolf and he tries to bite him and the porcupine is curled up underneath. He continues eating and then Nanabush sees him with the bushes on him and porcupine said I had to do something. Everybody is trying to eat me so I have to protect myself by putting these branches on my back. Nanabush says I will help you. Nanabush made a clay pack and put it on his back and he stripped the branches and put the thorns in the clay. So, the wolf sees the porcupine out there and tried to bite that clay pack and he got thorns stuck in his mouth and in his face and he runs away howling. Then the bear comes along and he sees the porcupine and thinks he would be a good meal so he takes a swipe at him and he runs away crying with thorns sticking out of his foot."

Second Legend

"Another story about how we got porcupines is told by Eli Thomas, who said, a long time ago in the village there was this man that always wanted to make war. He was always causing trouble. Always stirring up things. Then the people started to get fed up with him and then they told him, you should leave. You are not good for us. You're always causing trouble and always want to fight. You always want to hurt people. You should go and live in your own little village and make war. So, the man left. He went back to work again making weapons. So he said, I want to try these out. So, he went out there and shot the arrows up in the air and it went out of sight and he said 'this is great.' Shooting the rest of them up and a whole bunch more went up. And he heard a noise and looked up and here were all of these arrows and he realizes his mistake and there was no room to get out of the way. All those arrows fell on him and knocked him to the ground and he was on all fours. The arrows came down and landed on him and they stuck in him and that is the story."

Appendix 2 – History of Federal Indian Education Policy

Historical Events in Indian Education

"The Following is a chronological view of the development of Indian Education during the past 200 years. Since at least 1775, American Indians have had an ongoing, albeit tenuous relationship with the United States Government. While a concerted federal effort at educating the Indian has occurred only within the last fifty years, it has originated from the following historical events" (National Advisory Council on Indian Education, 1993).

1775 Continental Congress approves $500 to educate Indians at Dartmouth College

1778 September 17, 1778, the first treaty between the United States and an Indian Nation.

1802 Congress approves appropriations for Indian education not to exceed $15,000 annually "to provide civilization among the aborigines."

1818 Congress authorizes a civilization fund in the amount of $10,000 to convert Indians from hunters to agriculturalists.

1819 Congress passes a law on March 3, 1819, which states that the act was "designed to Provide against the further decline and final extinction of the Indian tribes adjoining The frontier settlements of the United States, and for introducing among them the habits and arts of civilization."

1870   Congress authorizes appropriations of $100,000 to operate federal industrial schools for Indians.

1871   Congress ends authority to make treaties with Indian tribes and nations.

1890   Federal tuition offered to public schools to educate Indian children.

1892   Congress authorizes the Commissioner of Indian Affairs to make and enforce regulations on Indian student attendance including the authority to withhold food and services from families that resist the "educational program" by refusing to send their children to school.

1906   Congress abolishes Oklahoma Cherokee school system.

1921   Congress passes the Snyder Act of 1921, which instructed the Secretary of Interior "to Direct, supervise, and expend such moneys as Congress may from time to time appropriate, for the benefit, care and assistance of Indians through the United States." The monies could be used for "general support and civilization, including education."

1928   Meriam Report to the Congress, which influenced a change in Indian education policies.

1934   Congress passes the Johnson O'Malley (JOM) Act, which authorizes contracts for welfare and educational services, and which was used to entice public school districts to assume more responsibility for providing an elementary and secondary education for Indian children who reside on Indian reservation lands.

1950   Congress amends Public Law 874 otherwise known as Impact Aid, which provides federal subsidies to public school districts to educate children residing on federal lands including Indian reservations.

1951 Congress passes a program to relocate Indians away from reservations.

1964 Congress passes Economic Opportunity Act, which provides for Indian children and adults to participate in Head Start, Upward Bound, Job Corps, Vista, and the Indian Community Action Program.

1965 Congress passes the Elementary and Secondary Education Act, which is intended to benefit socially and economically disadvantaged youth. Titles I and III of the act was amended to include Bureau of Indian Affairs (BIA) schools.

1966 Rough Rock Demonstration School, which is the first modern day Indian-controlled School funded by the federal government, opens within the Navajo Nation.

1967 Special Senate Subcommittee on Indian Education is established by Senate Resolution 165.

1968 Navajo Community College as the first tribally controlled Indian community college is Established in the Navajo Nation.

1969 Indian Education: A National Tragedy—A National Challenge, the Special Senate Subcommittee Report on Indian Education is released.

1970 Rama Navajo High School opens. It is the first Indian-controlled contract high school.

1971 Navajo Nation establishes the first comprehensive tribal education department, which contracts to administer the Bureau of Indian Affairs Office Title I Program and Higher Education Grants Program.

1972 Congress passes the Indian Education Act, which creates an Office of Indian Education Within the U.S. Office of Education, defines Indian to include members of state-recognized Indian tribes and descendents of Indians, establishes a quasi-entitlement program for Indians attending public schools, and establishes a National Advisory Council on Indian Education.

1975 Congress passes the Indian Self-Determination and Education Assistance Act, which opens up contacting.

1978 Congress passes the Indian Education Amendments, which establishes standards for BIA schools, institutionalizes BIA school boards, requires formula funding in BIA schools, and provides for increased Indian involvement in the use of Impact Aid funds.

1988 Congress passes Public Law 100-297, which reauthorize the Indian Education Act and calls for a White House Conference on Indian Education.

1989 Salt River Pima Maricopa Indian Community, through agreement with Mesa Public Schools (Arizona), gains control over Impact Aid.

1991 Indian Nations at Risk Task Force, created by Secretary of Education, issues its report.

1992 White House Conference on Indian Education held, resulting in 114 recommendations.

1993 The National Advisory Council on Indian Education recommends to the Congress that Indian education be a federal entitlement program (National Advisory Council on Indian Education, 1993).

Appendix 3 – Indian Affairs Head Apologized for Agency's Legacy of Racism

"WASHINGTON (AP) The head of the federal Bureau of Indian Affairs apologized for the agency's legacy of racism and in-humanity that included massacres, forced relocations of tribes and attempts to wipe out Indian languages and cultures.

"By accepting this legacy, we accept also the moral responsibility of putting things right, Kevin Gover, a Pawnee Indian said in an emotional speech Friday marking the agency's 175th anniversary. Gover said he was apologizing on behalf of the BIA, not the federal government as a whole. Still, he is the highest-ranking U.S. official ever to make such a statement regarding the treatment of American Indians.

"The audience of about 300 tribal leaders, BIA employees and federal officials stood and cheered as a teary-eyed Gover finished the speech. I thought it was a very heroic and historic moment, said Susan Masten, chairwoman of California's Yurok tribe and president of the National Congress of American Indians. Lloyd Tortalita, the governor of New Mexico's Acoma Pueblo tribe, welcomed the apology but said, If we could get an apology from the whole government, that would be better.

"Although Gover's statement did not come from the White House, President Clinton's chief adviser on Indian issues, Lynn Cutler, said Gover sent her a copy of his speech late Thursday and the White House did not object to it.

"Gover recited a litany of wrongs the BIA inflicted on Indians since its creation as the Indian Office of the War Department. Estimates vary widely, but the agency is believed responsible for the deaths of hundreds and thousands of Indians. This agency participated in the ethnic cleansing that befell the Western tribes, Gover said. It must be acknowledged that the deliberate spread of disease, the decimation of the mighty bison herds, the use of the poison alcohol to destroy mind and body, and the cowardly killing of women and children made for tragedy on a scale so ghastly that it cannot be dismissed as merely the inevitable consequence of the clash of competing ways of life.

"The miserly continued after the BIA became part of the Interior Department in 1849, Gover said. Children were brutalized in BIA-run boarding schools, Indian languages and religious practices were banned and traditional tribal governments were eliminated, he said. The high rates of alcoholism, suicide and violence in Indian communities today are the result, he said.

"Poverty, ignorance and disease have been the product of this agency's work, Gover said. Now, 90 percent of the BIA's 10,000 employees are Indian and the agency has changed into an advocate for tribal governments" (Sault Tribe News, 2000).

Appendix 4 – Informed Consent Form

We are seeking permission for you to participate in a research study. This study is designed as a part of a social work masters thesis. The results of this study are intended to provide more information about the boarding school experience and aftereffects.

The study involves a discussion of factors that many individuals face due to the Indian Boarding School experience. Participation in this study is completely voluntary. You may refuse to answer any question at any time. You may terminate the interview at any time. You may be contacted again, with your permission, if more information is needed.

You will remain anonymous. All data will be confidential between the researcher and the research project committee. The interviews will be tape recorded and transcribed by the researcher. All information will be stored in a locked cabinet and destroyed once the study is complete. Upon your request, you will receive a copy of the transcript of your interview.

You may ask for more information or clarification at any time. For more information, you should contact:

Professor Paul Hysenga, Chair
Research and Development Center
Grand Valley State University
201 Lake Michigan Hall
Allendale, MI 49401
Or Call Dr. Hysenga at 616-895-2025

I have read the above material and agree to voluntarily participate in the research study.

Participant:_____Date:_____

Signature of Witness: _____Date:_____

Appendix 5 – Research Questions

1. Tell me about your family of origin.

    A. Child rearing practices

    B. Ways of providing for family

    C. Traditional practices

    D. Religious practices (missionaries, spiritual practices, etc.)

2. What family customs from the past are still being practiced today by you and other family members.

3. Tell me about your boarding school experience.

    A. Relationships with family and others

    B. Perceptions of self

    C. Overall satisfaction with the quality of your life

    D. Typical day at the boarding school

Appendix 6 – History of the Meriam Report

The Meriam report, compiled after three years of field work, altered the congressional understanding of the condition and status of the Native Americans of all ages. Lewis Meriam was appointed as the technical director of the survey team referred to as the commission. An 847-page report was submitted to Hubert Work, the Secretary of the Interior, on February 21, 1928. The survey portrayed the ramifications of the Indian policy during the early part of the 20th century.

"In 1928, four years after the Citizenship Act, the government released the Meriam Report. The massive report excoriated the government's Indian policy and was the first comprehensive assessment of Indian life in the United States since Henry Rowe Schoolcraft was asked to undertake one in 1850. The appointment of the highly practical and unsentimental Lewis Meriam as lead investigator was something of a miracle for subjects who had, so often and for so long, been written about and advocated for by sensationalists who overlaid their real lives with meanings and significance that had little to do with them.

"For such a father of facts, however, precious few can be obtained about him or his views. He was born in Salem, Massachusetts, in 1883; took degrees at Harvard and George Washington universities; and received his Ph.D. from the Brookings Institution. He worked primarily as a statistician and did serious work for the Census Bureau before he was asked to conduct a study on the lives and living conditions of Indians across the country. He assembled a team of experts from different areas—health, education, law, economics, agriculture, and 'family life' among them. Once empaneled, the commission set out to see what was happening in Indian country, sometimes together and sometimes not, given the amount of ground they had to cover. Over a seven-month period, they visited ninety-five locations—reservations, hospitals, schools, and agencies—in twenty-two states. It would take the team another two and a half years to organize and analyze the data they collected. When they were done, they had managed to create a comprehensive, detailed, and impartial document that offered a damning assessment of how Indians had fared over the forty years the assimilation machine had been gobbling them up and churning out Americans.

"The report argued with facts and details, rather than passion and hyperbole, that federal Indian policy was a disaster. Health on reservations was as poor as it was in the boarding schools. Indians made, and continued to live on, much lower incomes than white Americans. Allotment had had a horrible effect on them. The allotments often couldn't support any farmers, much less those new to the enterprise. And whatever strategies had worked for Indians in more 'primitive' times had been supplanted by strategies that had been foisted on them and could not work where and how Indians actually lived. All in all, the report found that Indians were floundering on an American sea and were, as a whole, drowning.

"Lost in accounts of the years between 1918 and 1956 is the knowledge that the only reason there were any left at all was that they had fought. They had fought against the government, and they had fought with it. Deprived of every conceivable advantage or tool or clear-hearted advocate, they had continued to fight. Not just in the ways Dixon and people like him imagined, as warriors astride horses roaming free across the Plains, but rather as husbands and wives and fathers and mothers. As writers and thinkers. As farmers and soldiers in the Great War. But what to do when the actual fighting stops and the pressures bear down back home? What to do when you can't find the fight beyond the one for daily survival? What to do with that patrimony" (Truer. 2019, pgs. 201-202).

The survey revealed the hardships many Native Americans of all ages faced. For example, they discovered that young children did not belong in a boarding school. In order to ensure healthy development, children need to be with their families and their families need them. They should not be sent to boarding schools until they at least reached adolescence.

The government and missionaries did not study and gain an understanding of the Native Americans' religious practices and did not honor their traditional religious practices. Their dance practices may have appeared to be objectionable but white community activities also seemed foreign to the Native Americans. Another problem that surfaced consisted of their economic basis which has been destroyed by the encroachment of the white settlers. The Indian people could no longer make a living by hunting, fishing and gathering.

When the government adopted a policy of individual ownership of land with the expectation that Indians would become farmers, it failed miserably. It was discovered that many Indians did not live on the land allotted to them. The commission recommended the government needed to purchase land where the Indians wanted to reside.

The health of the Native Americans compared to the white population was poor. Accurate mortality and morbidity statistics were lacking at the time of the compilation of the report. The general death rate and infant mortality rates were high. Tuberculosis and Trachoma were the most prominent diseases.

The surveyors made the determination that the housing for many Native Americans was substandard. The government replaced traditional dwellings with small shacks with few rooms and inadequate provision for ventilation. They determined from a health standpoint that the traditional dwellings were often more sanitary than the permanent homes that have replaced them.

Often water had to be carried considerable distances from wells and natural springs. The supply of clean water was often inadequate. When the situation was improved by the government, their efforts were greatly appreciated (Wilson, 2018).

The status of many Native Americans has not improved. A multitude of Indian people still suffer from various health, educational and economical disparities.

Appendix 7 – The Doctrine of Discovery

Other players came into context when acts of land takeover and genocide occurred for the Native Americans. Roman Catholic popes established the Papal bull system, which involved an official papal letter or document with a seal (bulla) attached to the documents. Beginning in the 1400s, popes would designate a letter that presented a bulla, which represented the heads of apostles Peter and Paul on one side and the pope's signature on the other. These letters granted the authority for European explorers to take over sections of land from Native Americans. The letters were read to the native people in a language they did not understand and if they did not comply, the armed troops could do what they wanted to the native people. Pope Alexander VI submitted a papal bull to give Spain the authority to appoint missionaries to the Indies in 1493. Ferdinand and Isabella were granted full and free power, authority, and jurisdiction over most of the Americas via a papal bull (Rotondaro, 2015).

In 1823, a turning point occurred regarding a land dispute. A new type of property ownership was created for Native Americans during the U.S. Supreme Court case Johnson v. McIntosh. The Doctrine of Discovery was given a stamp of legitimacy. Chief Justice John Marshall's ruling stated:

"On the discovery of this immense continent, the great nations of Europe were eager to appropriate to themselves so much of it as they could respectively acquire. Its vast extent offered an ample field to the potentates of the old world found no difficulty in convincing themselves that they made ample compensation to the inhabitants of the new, by bestowing on them civilization and Christianity, in exchange for unlimited independence. But, as they were all in pursuit of nearly the same object, it was necessary, in order to avoid conflicting settlements, and consequent war with each other, to establish a principle, which all should acknowledge as the law by which the right of acquisition, which they all asserted, should be regulated as between themselves. This principle was, that discovery gave title to the government by whose subjects, or by whose authority, it was made, against all other European governments, which title might be consummated by possession," (Rotondaro, 2015, para. 14).

The ruling mandated that Native Americans, who were referred to as "fierce savages" and "the conquered" had the right to occupy the land without full sovereignty and tribal people must be dependent on the federal government.

"It may seem like papal statements from 500 years ago are ancient history. But Native American activists and scholars insist that Catholicism's past continues to affect the present. Papal bulls from the 1400s condoned the conquest of the Americas and other lands inhabited by indigenous people. The papal documents led to an international norm called the Doctrine of Discovery, which dehumanized non-Christians and legitimized their suppression by nations around the world, including by the United States. Now Native Americans say the church helped commit genocide and refuses to come to terms with it," (Rotondaro, 2015, para. 24).

Popes have given orders to take over land for centuries. A pope ordered soldiers to take over Jerusalem during the crusades. Many lost their lives such as whole villages of Jewish people. European soldiers stood outside of tribal villages in the developing country of the current United States and read documents that ordered the Indian people to surrender their land to the Anglo-invaders. Because the documents were in a language unknown to the Native Americans, they did not understand what was being read to them. In turn, the European interlopers committed heinous acts of genocide under the direction of the popes. They were given permission to murder the Indian people and disregarded one of the Ten Commandments "thou shall not kill." Throughout the history of this planet, the commandment to not kill was ignored if they felt the people to be killed were evil. Did the Native Americans fall into that category because of the color of their skin or was it because they lived differently?

Bibliography

Adams, D. (1995). *Education for Extinction: American Indians and the Boarding School Experience 1875-1928*. Kansas: University of Kansas Press.

Ambrose, S. (1996). *Undaunted Courage: Meriwether Lewis, Thomas Jefferson, and The Opening of the American West*. New York: Simon and Shuster Paperback.

American Indian Relief Council (N.D.). *History and Culture: Boarding Schools*. Retrieved from www.nativepartnership.org/site/PageServer?pagename=a-irc_hist_boardingschoolsServer?

Antone, R., Miller, D., Myers, B. (1986). *The Power Within People – A Community Organizing Perspective*. Canada: Peace Tree Technologies, Inc.

Bandura, A., (1973). *Aggression – A Social Learning Analysis*. New Jersey: Prentice Hall.

Banks, D. (2004). *Ojibwa Warrior: and the Rise of the American Indian Movement*. Norman: University of Oklahoma Press.

Benton-Banai, E., (1979). *The Mishomis Book -The Voice of the Ojibwe*. St. Paul: Indian Country Press, Inc.

Bierstedt, R., (1974). *Power and Progress - Essays on Sociological Theory*. New York: McGraw-Hill Book Company.

Bigelow, B. and Peterson, B., (Ed.). (1998). *Rethinking Columbus – The Next 500 Years*. Wisconsin: Rethinking Schools.

Bloom, J., (Spring, 1996). "Show What an Indian Can Do": Sports, Memory, and Ethnic Identity at Federal Indian Boarding

Schools. *Journal of American Indian Education*.V. 35, pp 33-48

Bordewich, F. (1996). *Killing the White Man's Indian*. New York: Anchor Books

Bouschor, B., (2001, July). Indians still failing to graduate. *Sault Tribe News*. p. 2

Bowden, H., (1981). *American Indians and Christian Missions – Studies in Cultural Conflict*. Chicago: The University of Chicago Press.

Bremer, R. (1987). *Indian Agent and Wilderness Scholar: The Life of Henry Rowe Schoolcraft*. Michigan Historical Society.

Brody, L. (Dec. 27, 2019). *Native Americans: The 12d Tribes of Michigan*. Retrieved From https://www.downtownpublications.com/single-post/2019/12/27NativeAmericans-the-12-tribes-of-Michigan.

Broker, I., (1983). *Night Flying Woman - An Ojibwe Narrative*. St. Paul: Minnesota Historical Society Press.

Brown, D., (1970). *Bury My Heart at Wounded Knee*. New York: Henry Holt and Company.

Brunner, S. (2021). *Beyond the Shadows: Addressing Historical Trauma*. Michigan: Freedom Eagles Press.

Brunner, S. (2021). *Manifest Destiny: A legacy of Genocide*. Michigan: Freedom Eagles Press.

Brunner, S. (2021). *Shadow Travelers: The Plight of Native Americans in Michigan After the European Invasion*. Michigan: Freedom Eagles Press.

Canavan, J., Dolan, P., and Pinkerton, J., (2000). Great Britain: Jessical Kingsley Publishers Ltd.

Champagne, D., (Ed.), (1994). *The Native American Almanac*. Detroit: Gale Research, Inc.

Child, B. (2000). *Boarding School Seasons: American Indian Families 1900-1940*. Nebraska: University of Nebraska Press.

Churchhill, W. (1997). *A Little Matter of Genocide: Holocaust and Denial in the Americas 1492 to the Present.* San Francisco: City Lights Books.

Churchhill, W. (2004). *Kill the Indian, Save the Man: The Genocidal Impact of American Indian Residential Schools.* San Francisco: City Light Books

Clarke Historical Society, (no date given). *Indian Treaties: Their Ongoing Importance to Michigan Residents.* Available [on-line] http:www.Lib.cmich.edu/clarke/nativeamericans/treatyrights/treattuition/htm

Cleland, C., (1992). *Rites and Conquests: The History and Culture of Michigan's Native Americans.* Ann Arbor: The University of Michigan Press.

Clifton, J., Cornell, G., and McClurken, J., (1986). *People of Three Fires – The Ottawa, Potawatomi, and Ojibwe of Michigan.* Grand Rapids: The Michigan Indian Press.

Conlan, R. (1994). *People of the Lakes: The Native Americans.* Virginia: Time Life Education.

Cornell, S., and Kalt, J., (1998). Sovereignty and Nation Building: The Development Challenge in Indian Country Today. *American Indian Culture and Research Journal.* v. 22, no. 3, pp. 187-214.

Crichton, James (Executive Producer). (1991). *In the White Man's Image.* [Film] (Available from PBS Video, 1320 Place, Alexandria, VA 22314-1698)

Danziger Jr., E., (1979). *The Chippewas of Lake Superior.* Norman: University Of Oklahoma Press.

Densmore, F. (1979). *Chippewa Customs.* Minnesota: Minnesota Historical Society Press.

Department of Health and Children, (Sept., 1999). *Children First - National Guidelines for the Protection and Welfare of Children.* Dublin: Brunswick Press Ltd.

Dunbar-Ortiz, R. (2014). *An Indigenous Peoples' History of the United States* .Boston: Beacon Press.

Eitzen, D., and Zinn, M., (1991). *In Confllict and Order - Understanding Society.* (5th ed.) Boston: Allyn and Bacon

Ehle, J., (1988). *Trail of Tears - The Rise and Fall of the Cherokee Nation.* New York: Anchor Books.

Ellis, J. (2007). *American Creation.* New York: Vintage Books.

Elizalde, T., Haywood, C., Ketchum, R. and VerHulst, M. (2015). *Indian Boarding Schools In Michigan.* Retrieved from https://umsi580.lsait.lsa.umich.edu/s/indian-boarding-Schools-in-michigan/page/authors.

Eyaa-keen Centre Inc. (2003). *Historic Traumatic Transmission (HTT): What is It?* Manitou, Canada: Eyaa-keen Centre, Inc.

Fixico, D., (2000). *The Urban Indian Experience in America.* Albuquerque: University of New Mexico Press.

Freire, P. (1993). *Pedagogy of the Oppressed.* New York: Continuum

Golder, E., and Kolker, K., (1994, July 17). Unholy Childhood - As Stories of a painfull past emerge, so too does hope for healing. *Grand Rapids Press.* pp 1-2.

Goodall, H., *Writing the New Ethnography.* Walnut Creek: Rowman and Littlefield Publishers, Inc.

Goodluck, C., (1993). Social Services with Native Americans - Current Status of the Indian Child Welfare Act. In H. McAdoo (Ed.), *Family Ethnicity Strength in Diversity.* London: Sage Publications.

Graham, L., (1995). *A Face in the Rock - A Tale of a Grand Island Chippewa.* London: University of California Press, Ltd.

Green, R., (1992). *Women in American Indian Society.* New York: Chelsea House Publishers.

Grinnell Jr., R., (1997). *Social Work Research and Evaluation – Quantitative and Qualitative Approaches.* (5th ed.) Illinois: F.E. Peacock Publishers, Inc.

Hanna, F., Talley, W., and Guindon, M., (Fall, 2000). The Power of Perception: Toward a Model of Cultural Oppression and Liberation. *Journal of Counseling and Development.* v. 78, issue 4, pages 430 – 441

Harjo, S., (1993). The American Indian Experience. In H. McAdoo (Ed.), *Family Ethnicity - Strength in Diversity.* London: Sage Publications.

Haviland, W., (1994). *Anthropology (7th ed.).* Florida. Holt, Rinehart and Winston, Inc.

Hilger, M., (1992). *Chippewa Child Life and Its Cultural Background.* St. Paul: Minnesota Historical Society Press.

Hogle, L. and Wilson, D., (1997). *Surviving in Two Worlds.* Austin: University Of Texas Press.

Holmes, T. (1996). *Strong Hearts/Wounded Souls: Native American Veterans of The Vietnam War.* Texas: University of Texas Press.

Horejsi, C., Craig, B., and Pablo, J., (1991). *Reactions by Native American Parents to Child Protection Agencies: A Look at Cultural and Community Factors.* Washington D.C: U.S. Department of Health and Human Services.

Hundleby, C., (1997). Where Standpoint Stands Now. In S. Kenney and H. Kinsella (Eds.) *Politics and Feminist Standpoint Theories.* New York: The Hawthorne Press, Inc.

Irving, D. (2018). *Waking Up White and Finding Myself in the Story of Race.* Massachusetts: Elephant Room Press.

Jambunathan, S., Burts, D., and Pierce, S., (Autumn, 2000). Comparisons of Parenting Attitudes Among Five Ethnic Groups in the United States. *Journal of Comparative Family Studies.* v. 31, no. 4, pages 395 -406

Johnson, B., (1990). *Ojibwe Ceremonies.* Lincoln: University of Nebraska Press.

Johnson, B., (1990). *Ojibwe Heritage.* Lincoln: University of Nebraska Press.

Johnson, T., (1997). *We Hold the Rock - This is Our Beginning of our Fight for Justice and Self-Determination.* San Francisco: Golden Gate National Parks Association.

Jones, B., (1999). *Indian Boarding Schools and the Indian Child Welfare Act.* [on-line] Available: nicwa.org/Pathways/page5.htm

Kemp, S., (1998). Practice with Communities. In M. Mattaini, Lowery, C. and Meyer, C. (Eds.), *The Foundation of Social Work Practice (*2nd ed., pp. 209-239) Washington D.C.: National Association of Social Workers.

Kolker, K., and Golder, E., (1994, July 17). Legacy of Shame. *Grand Rapids Press. pp 1-2.*

Lee, J., (1996). The Empowerment Approach to Social Work Practice. In F. Turner (Ed.), *Social Work Treatment.* (4th ed., pp. 218-249). New York: The Free Press.

Leigh, J. (1998). *Communicating for Cultural Competence.* Boston: Allyn and Bacon.

Leland, J., (1976). *Firewater Myths – North American Indian Drinking and Alcohol Addiction.* New Brunswick: Journal of Studies on Alcohol, Inc.

Lewis, J. (2000). *The Invasion. Michigan: Michigan State University Press.*

Littlefield, A., (1983). *Brief History of the Mt. Pleasant Indian Industrial School.* Mt. Pleasant: Anthropology Department, Central Michigan University

Littlefield, A., (1989). The B.I.A. Boarding School: Theories of Resistence and Social Reproduction. *Human and Society,* v. 13, no. 4, pp 428 - 441.

Littlefield, A., (1996). Indian Education and the World of Work in Michigan, 1893 - 1933. In A. Littlefield and M. Knack (Eds.). *Native Americans and Wage Labor - Ethnohistorical Perspectives.* Norman: University of Oklahoma Press.

Littlefield, H., (2001). *Children of the Indian Boarding Schools.* Minneapolis:Carolrhoda Books, Inc.

Littlefield, H., (2001). *Children of the Orphan Trains*. Minneapolis: Carolrhoda Books, Inc.

Locke, R., (1992). *The Book of the Navajo (5th ed.)*. Los Angeles: Mankind Publishing Co.

Loewen, J. (1995). *Lies My Teacher Told Me*. New York: Simon and Schuster.

Loewen, J. (1999). *Lies Across America - What Historic Sites Get Wrong*. New York: Simon and Schuster.

Loew, P., (1997). Hidden Transcripts in the Chippewa Treaty Rights Struggle: A Twice Told Tale; Story, Resistance, and the Politics of Power. *The American Indian Quarterly*. v. 21, no. 4, pp. 713-728.

Lomawaima, T. (Spring, 1996). Estelle Reel, Superintendent of Indian Schools, 1898 - 1910: Politics, Curriculum, and Land. *Journal of American Education*. v. 35, pages 5 - 31

Maracle, B. (1993). *Crazywater – Native Voice on Addiction and Recovery*. Toronto: Penguin Books.

Mason, W. (1998). Tribe and States: A New Era in Intergovernmental Affairs. *Publius*, v. 28, no. 1, pp. 111-130.

Matthiessen, P. (1991). *In the Spirit of Crazy Horse*. New York: Viking Press.

Meadows, K. (1990). *The Medicine Way – How to Live the Teachings of the Native American Medicine Wheel*. Shaftesbury, Dorset: Element.

Meadows, K., (1996). *Earth Medicine – Revealing the Hidden Teachings of the Native American Medicine Wheel*. Shaftesbury, Dorset: Element.

Medicine, E. (1991). *Buffalo Woman Comes Singing*. New York: Ballantine Books.

Mehojah, W. (September 6, 2000). *S. 2580, the Indian School Construction Act*. Washington, D.C.: U.S. Department of the Interior

Mehta, S. (2019). *This Land is Our Land: An Immigrant's Manifesto*. New York: Farrar, Straus and Giroux.

Miller, J. (1996). *Shingwauk's Vision: A History of Native Residential Schools*. Toronto: University of Toronto Press.

Nabigon, H. and Mawhiney, A. (1996). Aboriginal Theory - A Cree Medicine Wheel Guide for Healing - First Nations. In F. Turner (Ed.), *Social Work Treatment*. (4th ed., pp. 18-38). New York: The Free Press.

Napier, D. (May, 2000). *Sins of the Fathers. Anglican Journal*. 16 Page Special Report.

National Advisory Council on Indian Education, (1993). *Indian Education: A Federal Entitlement*. Washington, D.C.: National Advisory Council on Indian Education.

The National Native American Boarding School Healing Coalition (N.D.) *Truth and Healing Commission on Indian Boarding School Policies Act*. Retrieved from boardingshcoolhealing.org/truthcommission

Native American Partnership, (May 16, 2013). *The Termination Era*. Retrieved from www.nativepartnership.org/site/PageServer?pagename=PWN ANative History terminationpolicvNP.

Native Children Have High Rate of Neglect and Abuse, (2001, April).*Sault Tribe News. p. 4.*

Neihardt, J. (1972). *Black Elk Speaks*. Lincoln: University of Nebraska Press.

Nies, J. (1996). *Native American History: A Chronology of a Culture's Vast Achievements and Their Links to World Events*. New York: Ballantine Books.

Nobokow, P. (1999). *Native American Testimony: A Chronicle of Indian-White Relations From Prophecy to the Present*. New York: Penguin Books.

Otto, S. (1990). *Walk in Peace - Legends and Stories of the Michigan Indians*. Sault Ste. Marie: The Michigan Indian Press Sault Ste. Marie Tribe of Chippewa Indians

Paquin, R. and Doherty, R. (1992). *Not First in Nobody's Heart - The Life of a Contemporary Chippewa.* Iowa: Iowa State University Press.

Partnership With Native Americans, (2015). *Living Conditions (Reservations).* Retrieved from www.nativepartnership.org/site/PageServer?pagename=Naa_livingconditions.

Podles, S. (2008). *Sacrilege: Sexual Abuse in the Catholic Church.* Maryland: Crossland Press.

Prusha, S. (2000). *Documents of United States Indian Policy.* Nebraska: University of Nebraska Press.

Reinhardt, Martin (1998). *The Pre-Legislative History of the Michigan Indian Tuition Waiver.* Master's Thesis, Central Michigan University, Mt. Pleasant, Michigan

Richard, J. (2000, November). *Lessons in Fear. People Weekly.* v. 54, pp 192 - 194.

Rinaldi, A. (1999). *My Heart is on the Ground - The Diary of Nannie Rose, a Sioux Girl - Carlisle Indian School, Pennsylvania, 1880.* New York: Scholastic Inc.

Reyner, J. and Eder, J. (2004). *American Indian History:* Oklahoma: *University Of Oklahoma Press.*

Robinson-Zanartu, C. and Majel-Dixon, J. (Fall, 1999). Parent Voices: American Indian Relationships with Schools. *Journal of American Indian Education.* v. 36, Pages 33 – 54

Rotondaro, E. (2001). *Disastrous doctrine had papal roots.* Retrieved from http:// www.ncronlineorg/news/justice/disastrous-had-papal-roots.

Rothernberg, P. (1998). *Race, Class, and Gender in the United States – An Integrated Study.* (4th ed.) New York: St. Martin's Press

Rotter, J., Chance, J., and Phares, E., (1972). *Applications of a Social Learning Theory of Personality.* New York: Holt, Rinehart and Winston, Inc.

Rushton, J. (1980). *Altruism, Socialization, and Society.* New Jersey: Prentice-Hall, Inc.

Saleeby, D. (1997). *The Strengths Perspective in Social Work Practice.* (2nd ed.) New York: Longman.

Sanchez, J., and Stuckey, M. (Summer, 1999). From Boarding Schools to the Multicultural Classroom: The Intercultural Politics of Education, Assimilation, and American Indians. *Teacher Education Quarterly,* v. 26, no. 3, pages 83 –96

Sault Tribe News. (September, 2000). *Indian Affairs head apologized for agency's "legacy of racism"* p. 3.

Sault Ste. Marie Tribe of Chippewa Indians (no date available). *The Story of a People.* [Film] (Available from the Sault Ste. Marie Tribe of Chippewa Indians Video Production Department and the Communications Department, 206 Greenough St., Sault Ste. Marie, MI 49783)

Schaef, A. (1995). *Native Wisdom for White Minds: Daily Relections Inspired by Native Peoples of the World.* New York: Ballantine Books.

Sharpes, D. (1979). *Federal Education for the American Indians.* Journal for American Indian Education: Arizona State University. Retrieved from http://jaie.asu.edu/v19/v19S1fed.htm.

Standefer, A. (1999, December). The Federal Juvenile Delinquency Act:A Disparate Impact on Native American Juveniles. *Minnesota Law Review.* v. 84, no. 2, Pages 473 - 503

Stanton, A. (July 7, 2008). *Wounded Souls.* Retrieved from http://www.northernexpress.com/editorial/features.asp?id=3241

Steffen, C. (1999). *Dancing Through the Darkness – The Cognitive Treatment Of Shame.* Illinois: Realizing Potentials Press.

Stout, M. and Kipling, G. (2003). *Aboriginal People: Resilience and the Residential School Legacy.* Ontario: Aboriginal Healing Foundation.

Strickland, R. (Editor-in-Chief) (1982). *F. Cohen, Handbook of Federal Indian Law.* Charlottesville, Virginia: Michie Bobbs-Merrill Law Publishers.

Sugden, J. (1997). *Tecumseh: A Life*. New York: Henry Holt and Company.

Tancredo, (April 3, 2001). *107th Congress - 1st Session - H. Con. Res. 95 -Supporting a National Charter Schools Week.* [online] :

Tanner, H. (1992). *The Ojibwa*. New York: Chelsea House Publishers.

Taylor, L. (September, 1995). *Rebirth. Canada and the World Backgrounder*. v. 61, Pages 4 – 7

The National Native American Boarding School Coalition (N.D.). *U.S. Indian Boarding School History*. Retrieved from http://boardingschoolhealing.org/education/us/-indian-boarding-school-history.

Thoma, R. (1997). *Special Report: Under Seige - The Indian Child Welfare Act of 1978.*
Retrieved from: Home.rica.net/rthoma/icwa.htm

Treuer, D. (2019). *The Heartbeat of Wounded Knee: Native America from 1890 to the Present*. New York: Riverhead Books.

Tyler, S. (1973). *The History of Indian Policy*. Washington, D.C.: United States of the Interior Bureau of Indian Affairs.

U.S. Commission on Civil Rights, (2018). *Broken Promises: Continuing Federal Funding Shortfall for Native Americans.* Retrieved from https://www.usccr.gov/files/pubs/2018/12-20-Broken-Promises.pdf

Van Alstine, R. (March 18, 1994). *Historical Development of Sault Ste. Marie Tribe of Chippewa Indians and Evolution of Education at Bahweting*. Sault Ste. Marie: Bureau of Indian Affairs.

Van Alstine, R., Reinhardt, M., and Owens, E., (October 31, 1994). *The Bureau of Indian Affairs Minneapolis Area Office of Indian Education Programs Manual on Area Tribes, Tribal Schools, Community Colleges and Inter-Tribal Councils.* Sault Ste. Marie: Bureau of Indian Affairs Michigan Agency OIEP

Welton, N. (1997). Nancy Hartsock's Standpoint Theory: From Content to "Concrete Multiplicity." In S. Kenney and H. Kinsella (Eds.) *Politics and Feminist Standpoint Theories.* New York: The Hawthorne Press, Inc.

Wilson, B. (2018). *Congress Whispers, Reservation Nations Endure. 2nd Edition.* Ohio: B.L. Wilson Associates, LLC

Wilson, J. (1998). *The Earth Shall Weep - A History of Native America.* New York: Grove Press.

Wise, J. (1971). *The Red Man in the New World Drama - The great classic of the political and legal history of the American Indian.* New York: MacMillan.

About the Author

Sharon Brunner, an enrolled member of the Sault Ste. Marie Tribe of Chippewa Indians (Sault Tribe), is a storyteller who writes about Native Americans from all over the U.S. and in Michigan. She has published three other books associated with the history of the Native Americans in the U.S. and Michigan and published a self-help book addressing historical trauma. In 2002, she earned a Masters of Social Work degree with an emphasis placed on Indian child welfare from Grand Valley State University. The thesis project submitted for this literary project was completed as a requirement for this degree. Sharon was a former federal reviewer for the Department of Health and Human Services out of Washington D.C. reviewing Head Start programs throughout the U.S., mostly tribal programs. She was a college professor for the Bay Mills Community College, a tribal college in Brimley, Michigan and she was employed as an education manager for the Sault Tribe for many years. Sharon served on a Child Welfare Committee for the Sault Tribe for over twenty-three years which addressed the hardships many of the Ojibwe families were facing. She has over thirty years of experience with providing services to Native Americans.

www.ingramcontent.com/pod-product-compliance
Lightning Source LLC
Chambersburg PA
CBHW070552160426
43199CB00014B/2477